# Living and In'
# in the "Neu

A guide to inexpensive living and making money in the (aribbean's most beautiful tropical paradise

## Written by
## CHRISTOPHER HOWARD

# LIVING AND INVESTING IN THE "NEW" CUBA

By
Christopher Howard

## Second Edition

Edited by
Dr. Daniel Spitzer

Photos courtesy of Bill Baker and Robert Hodel

Published in Costa Rica by
© 2001-2002 Astro Corporation, Inc.

**ISBN 1-881233-51-0**
**Costa Rica Books**
**Suite # 1  SJO 981**
**P.O. Box 025216**
**Miami, FL 33102-5216**
www.costaricabooks.com  www.liveincuba.com
**E-mail: crbooks@racsa.co.cr**

iv

# WHAT THE EXPERTS ARE SAYING ABOUT THIS BOOK

"What a timely book! This INTERESTING new guidebook provides A LOT OF food for thought about Cuba's future and the many opportunities which may await foreigners."

*-Jens Jurgen,*
*Travel Tips + News,*
*North America's Foremost Travel Newsletter*

"INDISPENSABLE for anyone eyeing Cuba as an investment opportunity or a place to live."

*- Christopher Baker,*
*Havana Handbook 2000*

"Living and Investing in the New Cuba ia a SUPERB guide to living, making money and creating the good life in Cuba."

*- James Cox,*
*The Midwest Book Review*

"This is the FIRST guide about living and investing in Cuba. It paints a REALISTIC picture of what life may be like in Cuba of the future."

*- JayTrettien,*
*Central America Weekly*

"A PERFECT compliment to The Cuba and Havana Handbooks."

*- Destination Cuba*

"This is the most beautiful land that human eyes have ever seen."

*Christopher Columbus upon setting foot on the island of Cuba in 1492.*

# ACKNOWLDGEMENTS

This second edition would not have become a reality without the invaluable help of many people.

I would first like to thank my graphic designer, William "El Mago" Morales, for his hard work and patience.

I am also very grateful to Robert and Steven Hodel, the owners of Destination Cuba, for the invaluable information and contacts they provided.

A special thanks to Jay Trettien and Dr. Daniel Spitzer for their  contributions to this edition.

I would also like to thank Christopher Baker, author of the  best-selling Cuba Handbook  and award-winning Costa Rica Handbook, and  Moon Publications  for their help.

I  am indebted to Mary de Waal, for her inspiration and support.

I would like to acknowledge all of the assistance I have received from the Publishers Marketing Association's book promotional programs.  Thanks to them, this  book will soon  be sold in most major bookstores in the U.S. and Canada.

Finally, I would like to express my eternal gratitude to members of my family, especially my late mother,  for their constant support when I needed it the most.

Christopher Howard
San José, Costa Rica

# ABOUT THE AUTHOR

The author, Christopher Howard, has written the highly acclaimed travel guide, *The New Golden Door to Retirement and Living in Costa Rica*. His most recent work is the visionary *Living and Investing in the New Nicaragua*. Mr. Howard has lived and traveled extensively in Mexico, Central and South America. Therefore, it is not surprising that he has first-hand knowledge and insight into all aspects of living in Latin America.

Furthermore, he has a foreign language background, having earned a B.A. in Spanish and Latin American Studies from the University of California at Los Angeles, and a Masters Degree in Spanish from the University of California. He also has a credential to teach Spanish at all levels from California State University, San Francisco.

Mr. Howard was the recipient of scholarships for graduate study at the University of the Americas in Puebla, Mexico and the Jesuit University of Guadalajara, Mexico.

**The author in front of his new home in Lagunilla de Heredia.**

He has been a columnist for the newspapers Costa Rica Today and *Central America Weekly*, the award-winning newsletter, *Costa Rican Outlook* and the Costa Rican Resident's Association magazine, *El Residente*. He is currently a paid consultant for *National Geographic* and working on a screenplay which takes place in Central America.

Mr. Howard resides in San José Costa Rica with his Costa Rican wife and 12 year old son. He is one of the few writers of travel guides about Latin America who lives there full time.

# CONTENTS

Introduction

## Chapter 1
### Why Cuba?

## Chapter 2
### An Introduction to Cuba. What is Cuba?

## Chapter 3
### Exploring Cuba

## Chapter 4
### Places to Go and Things to Do

# Chapter 5
## Short Cuts for Learning Spanish

# Chapter 6
## Living in Cuba

# Chapter 7
## Saving Money

# Chapter 8
## Making Money

# Chapter 9
## Getting There, Moving There and Staying There

# Chapter 10
## Useful Information

# FOREWORD

All of us, at one time or another, have imagined leaving the rat race, saying to hell with everything and realizing our dreams by moving to our own paradise.

Whether you are of retirement age, a burned out baby boomer, or seasonal traveller, this book should provide you with food for thought and sufficient information to start you on the journey to beginning a new life in Cuba.

For over 40 years Cuba has been isolated from the mainstream of the world while trying to live the socialist dream. The world has changed and so has Cuba. Now is the moment to come and explore the country that has so much to offer. Whether you are someone interested in wintering or just want to live part or full-time in Cuba or a savvy entrepreneur, this guidebook will help you. It paints a realistic picture of living in a Latin American country and tells you how to deal with the many challenges you will inevitably have to confront.

This guide offers assistance to anyone seeking a safe, affordable place to live outside of the United States and Canada. It contains all of the ins and outs, dos and dont's, rules of thumb, secret insider information and invaluable data about all aspects of living in Cuba. It shows you how to stay busy, where to reside, how to learn Spanish, where to find companionship. It provides you with novel, sure-fire ideas for starting businesses and, best of all, gives you a head start before you even move to Cuba.

Cuba is the most populous and largest island in the Caribbean. Located only 90 miles from the U.S. mainland, Cuba—sometimes called the "Pearl of the Caribbean" for its beauty—boasts miles and miles of breathtaking terrain, towering mountains, spectacular landscapes, quaint colonial towns and a couple of cosmopolitan cities. The 300-odd unspoiled beaches, bays and inlets surrounded by the beautiful crystal-clear waters of the Caribbean have always been the island's main attraction.

The country's subtropical climate with 300 days of sunshine, low cost of living for residents, an abundance of outdoor activities, towns and cities steeped in history and the friendly funloving  nature of the people, all contribute to its limitless appeals, making it a dream waiting to come true.

The rich flora of the countryside and the scent of tropical flowers always fill the air.  Singing tropical birds, butterflies and an abundance of exotic species  serve to attract droves of nature lovers.  World class scuba diving and sportsfishing draw sportsman to the island.

The city of Havana is the heart of the country.  Havana is the most impressive city in the Caribbean.  It was always the closest place Americans would visit for every imaginable type of entertainment from cockfights to gambling.  Colonial Havana is a monument to sixteenth century architecture and contrasts with the modern part of the city.  The city of Trinidad is another colonial gem.  World renowned resorts such as Varadero, visitor and are easily accessible.

Guardalavaca and Key Largo—to name a few— beckon the visitor and are easily accessible.

Cuba offers something for every imaginable taste and lifestyle. *Trends Magazine* predicted that Cuba would someday become the baby boomer's retirement haven of the future.   A June 1998 issue of the *Miami Herald* stated, "A mass new migration of retirees will start to settle abroad, lured by the low cost of living to stretch their shrinking pensions, reasonable health costs and warm weather.  Cuba will be the *hottest* destination due to its proximity to the United States and the relative lack of industrialization."

Cuba is ripe for entrepreneurs since foreign investment is now welcome and small enterprise is beginning to flourish. The country's 12 million people constitute the largest potential market in the region. Canadians and Europeans are pouring capital into the country since investment laws have been relaxed. The country's new investment law allows foreign businessmen to own businesses, their offices and housing. Cuba has left the cold war behind and is now ready to participate in the emerging global economy. The Cuban government realizes the time has come to participate in the new world economic order. The country is now ripe for the international investors who want to start new businesses.

It is now time to get your foot in the door before the gold rush begins and hordes of entrepreneurs carve up the island completely. There will be unprecedented invesment opportunity awaiting you in the not-too-distant future. So, now is the moment for adventurous individuals to reap the tremendous opportunities which may await them in Cuba. Furthermore, in the last 10 years a few of the reforms made to the Cuban economy create limited self-employment, legalize the use of U.S. dollars and encourage foreign banking and investment.

Additional advantages for foreign investors are a highly educated, well-disciplined labor force, tremendous opportunities in tourism's untapped areas and an improving infrastructure

Non-U.S. foreigners have been enjoying this paradise for the last couple of decades. It will soon be your turn. Come to Cuba and start a new and exciting life. Take advantage of all of the wonders this beautiful country has to offer.

Conditions for investing and living in Cuba are improving. Nobody can foresee the future with absolute certainty. However, given the events of the last couple of years and the direction the country is currently moving, predictions we make in this book are inevitable. Cuba cannot afford to be left out of the mainstream of world progress. The Chinese, Vietnamese and formerly communist European nations have realized this and are opening their markets to the world. Now it's Cuba's turn to do the same. Whether change will come tomorrow or even this year is hard to foretell, but it will occur. Just be patient, ready to act and to use the information in this guidebook.

# Cuba General Information

| | |
|---|---|
| **Capital** | La Havana (pop. 2,090,000) |
| **Population** | 11,500,000(1999) |
| **Size** | 42,804 square miles |
| **Quality of Life** | Good (excellent weather, lacking some comforts, friendly people) |
| **Official Language** | Spanish (some people speak English) |
| **Political System** | Independent socialist republic |
| **Currency** | Peso (the US dollar used widely) |
| **Investment Climate** | Joint venture opportunities with some private ownership |
| **Official Religion** | None but Catholicism and Santería are also practiced |
| **Foreign Population** | Over 30,000 |
| **Longevity** | 75 years (higher than the US) |
| **Literacy** | 98% (highest in Latin America) |
| **Time** | Central Standard (U.S.) |

# THINGS TO THINK ABOUT BEFORE MOVING TO A NEW COUNTRY OR MAKING FOREIGN INVESTMENTS

❑ What is required to become a legal resident? Can I meet these requirements? What is the cost? How often does residency have to be renewed, what are the conditions of renewal and what is the cost?

❑ What is required to visit, or while you are waiting for residency?

❑ What is the political situation? How stable is the country?

❑ Weather ( Do you like the year-round weather?)

❑ Income taxes (Are you taxed on income brought into the country? Are you allowed to earn income in the country? If yes, How is it taxed?

❑ Other taxes? ( Sales tax, import duties, exit taxes, vehicle taxes, etc.)

❑ How much will it cost in fees, duties and other taxes to bring your personal possessions into the country? (Cars, boats, appliances, electronic equipment, etc.)

❑ Rental property - How much? Availability?

❑ Purchase property - Property taxes, restrictions on foreign ownership of property, expropriation laws, building regulations, squatters rights, etc. Is there a capital gains tax?

❑ Communications - Are there reliable phone and fax lines, cellular phones, beepers, connections to Internet and other computer communication service? Is there good mail service between the country and the rest of the world? Are there private express mail services like DHL and FEDEX? Are there local newspapers, radio and TV in a language you understand? Is there cable or satellite TV available?

❑ Transportation - How are the roads? Are flights available to places you want to go? How are the buses and taxis ? How costly is it to travel to and from your chosen country to frequent destinations?

❑ Is it difficult for friends and family to visit you?

❑ Shopping - Are replacement parts available for the items you have brought from home? If so, what are the costs? If not, how much will it cost to import what you need?

❑ Are the types of foods you are accustomed to readily available in both markets and restaurants?

❑ If you have hobbies, are clubs, supplies and assistance available?

❑ What cultural activities are available? (Art, music, theatre, museums, etc.)

❑ What entertainment is available? (Sports, movies, night clubs, dancing, etc.)

❑ What recreational facilities are available? (Golf courses, tennis, health clubs, recreational centers, parks, etc.)

❑ If you like the beach, are good beaches available? Can they be reached easily? What is the year round temperature of the water?

❑ What is the violent crime rate? Minor crime (theft, car and house break-ins)? What support can be expected from the police department; Are the police helpful to foreign residents?

❑ How do local residents treat foreign visitors and residents?

❑ What are the local investment opportunities? Is there any consumer or investment protective legislation for investors? What return can you expect from your investments? Is the local help reliable? What regulations are involved in hiring employees? What are the employer's responsibilities to the workers?

❑ Is the banking system safe and reliable? Can they transfer funds and convert foreign currency, checks, drafts, and transfers? Are checking, savings and other accounts you may need available to foreigners? Is there banking confidentiality? Is there a favorable rate of exchange with the U.S. dollar?

❑ Are good lawyers, accountants, investment advisors and other professionals available?

❑ How difficult is it to start a business and what kind of opportunities are there?

❑ How is the health care system? Is it affordable? Do they honor U.S. and Canadian health insurance? Are there any diseases which are dangerous to foreigners, and does the local health care system address the problem? What is the quality of hospitals, clinics, doctors and dentists? What is the availability of good specialists?

❑ How is the sanitation? Can you drink the water? Do the restaurants have good sanitation standards? Are pasteurized milk and other dairy products available? Do meat, fish, and vegetable markets have satisfactory sanitary standards?

❑ If you are interested in domestic staff, what is the cost of cooks, housekeepers and gardeners, etc.?

❑ What legislation is there to protect foreign residents? What rights do foreign residents have in comparison to citizens?

# CHAPTER 1

## WHY CUBA?

Aside from its beauty and low cost of living, the most compelling reason for living in Cuba is its convenient location. The country is only about 100 miles from U.S. mainland — making it very accessible.

Tropical Cuba is really closer to the U.S. than Mexico's best vacation sites. One has to travel hundreds of miles into Mexico to find good resorts, tropical climates and the best area to live—northern Mexico is dry in the summer and very cold in the winter. Nearby resorts like barren Ensenada and Rosarito in Baja California are no match for Cuba's tropical beauty. In addition, Mexico has lost much of its appeal as a retirement haven in recent years due to a number of factors. At present the country rates a close second to Columbia when it comes to violence, corruption, kidnappings, drug trafficking, recurrent economic woes, assassinations and general political instability. The kidnapping of both foreigners and Mexican citizens has risen in recent times. The police seem be be more violent and dishonest than the criminals—often extorting foreigners because they are easy prey.

Forget doing business in Mexico. The financial climate is unpredictable due to the current economic crisis and devaluations. Most investment opportunities are drying up. On top of that, any foreigner who has ever tried to start a business there will tell you the red tape and payoffs seem unending. Couple all this with the tension between the U.S. and Mexico over drug traffic and unbridled illegal immigration and you have a country that is no longer conducive to long-term living let alone retirement or for starting a business.

America's tropical paradise, Hawaii, is 6 hours away by plane and prohibitively expensive. Cuba's Varadero resort is considered by many to be just as beautiful as Hawaii.

Because of Cuba's proximity to the States it was the playground and perennial escape for Americans before the revolution of 1959. In the old days people would flock to the island by boat, plane and even in private yachts for a few days of fun and pleasure. There were also many Americans and other foreigners living there on a permanent basis. The most famous expatriate was Ernest Hemingway.

Once the country is completely accessible to Americans you will have the option of living there on a full or part-time basis. It is comforting to know you will be able to return to the States quickly in the event of an emergency or other personal business— Miami is only 30-minutes away by air. Such closeness also tends to reduce the feeling of isolation that affect many people when they leave their own country to move to a foreign land. Friends and relatives will be able visit you easily. This proximity provides easy access to U. S. culture in case one gets homesick. Miami TV and radio stations can be picked up from Havana and other nearby areas, giving you a quick fix of U. S. culture.

A trip to Cuba is really like travelling between two U.S. cities. Eventually you will be able to go shopping, visit friends or take care of business in Miami and return the same day. You will even be able to commute back and forth if you really needed to—making it ideal for some businessmen.

Ask many people why they would like to live in Cuba, and its mild tropical climate is usually near the top of the list. Canadians, Europeans and others have been flocking to Cuba for years to escape harsh winters. They can be found basking in the sun at any of the island's beach resorts. As we alluded to in a previous section, Cuba has around 300 days of sunshine each year.

Cuba is also a healthy place to live. The county's salubrious climate agrees with most people. Cuba's longevity rate is as high as most developed countries—making it one of the healthiest countries in the world.

This healthy life-style is in part due to Cuba's first-rate health care system. Doctors are well-trained and medical facilities are good. Much innovative research has been done in Cuba. Foreigners can be sure of receiving excellent health care. However, if you don't feel comfortable with Cuba's health care system it will be easy to see a U.S. doctor since Florida is so near. In situations requiring specialized care and treatment you may have the option of returning home.

Another compelling reason for living in Cuba is the country's friendly people. They are warm, hospitable, fun-loving people famous for their sense of humor and knowing how to enjoy life and getting together for song and dance. Many will even take you into their homes to meet their families. Despite the poor relations with the U.S. in recent years, the average Cuban will treat U.S. citizens courteously.

In Cuba there is plenty to do— something for everyone and everything for someone. Because the island is so large there are many sights to see, places to explore and a myriad of exciting activities to keep a person busy—especially in and around Havana. You won't be bored unless you are just plain lazy. It will be easy to lead an active lifestyle. Speaking of lifestyles, if you are tired of the hustle bustle and rat race you will find it easy to adopt Cuba's more laid back way of living. Whether you live there full or part-time, you will enjoy the slow pace.

The affordability of the country is another plus. Like most third world countries the cost of living for residents is relatively low when compared to the U.S., Canada or Europe. Housing, utilities, transportation and food will be bargains. If you have dollars, your money will go even farther. Domestic help will be inexpensive. It will be possible to hire servants for modest wages to do cooking, cleaning, gardening, babysitting and a multitude of other tasks. This will free you to have more time to yourself and enjoy all that Cuba has to offer.

Although some cracks have appeared in the political system in recent years due to a poor economy, the country is stable. For almost forty years the government has endured in its present form. Not many third world countries have enjoyed this kind of stability — indeed a rare phenomenon in Latin America. Only Costa Rica can make a similar claim.

There is by far less crime in Cuba than in the U.S. or neighboring Caribbean countries. Like every country in the world, Cuba does have some crime. No society is crime free. However, violent crime is rare. Penalties are harsh and serve as a powerful deterrent. There is a lot of petty crime and theft. As in other places, the countryside is more crime free than urban areas.

As we alluded to in the foreword , there are a wealth of possibilities for the energetic entrepreneur in Cuba. There is also a huge consumer market of nearly 12,000,000 people waiting to be tapped. Cubans have been aware of most American products and brand names for many years. In fact, many U.S. goods are already being sold on the black market . Everything from Campell's Soup to Nike are presently available.

All of the above factors, plus such intangibles as the sensuality of the island, its mystic, tropical flavor, incredible vistas, prospect of making new friends, exciting adventures that await you, best beaches in the Caribbean and so much more, will make Cuba the ideal place to live. So, be prepared to enjoy Cuba in all its splendor.

# CHAPTER 2

## AN INTRODUCTION TO CUBA: WHAT IS CUBA?

### The Lay of the Land

Cuba is the largest and most populous island in the Caribbean sea. The Atlantic Ocean is to the north and the Caribbean Sea to the south. The island lies almost south of the Tropic of Cancer at the mouth of the Gulf of Mexico. The province of *Pinar del Río* is about 120 miles northeast of Mexico's Yucatan Peninsula while *Havana* is around 100 miles south of Key West Florida, 48 miles west of Haiti and 87 miles north of Jamaica. Santiago de Cuba is located 180 miles northeast of Jamaica.

The island's shape resembles that of an alligator. It is about 775 miles long,—approximately the same distance from New York to Chicago— and ranges in width from 25 to 120 miles. The area of the island is 44,218 square miles (110,860 sq. km). About 60 percent of the land is flat fertile plains, used for cattle grazing and growing sugar cane.

Forested mountains make up a quarter of Cuba's territory. There are three main mountain areas, one at each end of the country and a third in the south central region. The *Sierra Maestra* , located at the eastern end of Cuba, has the most rugged terrain and is Cuba's most spectacular mountain range. It has been the scene of several guerilla uprisings. The highest peak in the range is the *Pico Turquino* which rises to 6,540 feet. The Trinidad mountains are part of the *Sierra Escambry* in the center of the island and are only 3,000 feet at their highest point. The *Sierra de los Organos* in western Cuba, where unique knolls called *mogotes*, or buttes, rise from the floor of the Viñales Valley, got its name because it looked like the pipes of an organ to the Spanish conquerors. These mountains and the *Sierra del Rosario* are both part of the *Cordillera de Guaniguanico* mountain range.

Cuba's 2,200 miles of jagged coastline has hundreds of alluring beaches and 200 bays. It also has around 4,195 keys and islets. The island is divided into 14 geographically different provinces plus the Island of the Youth or *Isla de Juventud*, formerly called the Island of the Pines or *La Isla de los Pinos*. From east to west, the population centers are *Santiago de Cuba, Guantánamo, Holguín, Granma, Las Tunas, Camagüey, Ciego de Avila, Santi Spíritus, Cienfuegos, Villa Clara, Matanzas*, the Province of Havana, the City of Havana and *Pinar del Río*—the tobacco growing region.

## (limate

Cuba's weather is pleasant and subtropical. The island lies in a tropical zone, but trade winds of the ocean and warm currents from the gulf stream keep the climate moderate, and less extreme than as in other tropical areas.

There are only two seasons, the dry season or la estación seca , from November to early May, and the rainy season or, la estación lluviosa, from May to October. It rains every day in the summer. Relative humidity is 77 percent during the dry season and 82 percent in the rainy season.

Showers can last up to an hour and are usually followed by sunshine and blue skies. Speaking of sun —there is an average eight hours of sunlight daily and 300 sunny days throughout the year.

There are no pronounced seasonal variations in temperature. The average temperature is around 77°F /25°C. Humidity and rainfall are the highest in September or October. July and August are the hottest months with temperatures averaging 89°F /32°C. The coldest months tend to be January and February. September is the wettest month and February and March tend to be the driest. There is no danger of frost in Cuba since the lowest temperature is around 45°F. The average annual temperature of Havana is approximately 77°F/25.2°C with summer highs of 82°F/25.8°C. The ideal time to visit the country is between March and May.

The climate varies from region to region. The mountains are cooler with the south and east being drier and warmer. In general the eastern provinces are warmer than the western ones except in the mountain areas.

Cuba lies in an area that is subject to hurricanes. The hurricane season runs from June to November with the worst storms in September or October. There have been a few big hurricanes this century that have affected Cuba. Havana and Pinar del Río are usually more susceptible than the eastern provinces. However, you should not lose any sleep over the prospect of hurricanes. They don't occur on a regular basis and you are usually given ample warning to take adequate measures to protect yourself.

Because of Cuba's warm tropical climate you can feel comfortable wearing casual cotton clothing during the day. However at night, you may be required to dress-up for going to restaurants or nightclubs.

# Flora and Fauna

Plants and wildlife abound in Cuba. There are over 8,000 species of plants, 200 species of butterflies and 300-odd bird species. The island's lakes are home to quail, pheasant and migratory ducks. The Zapata Peninsula, near the Bay of Pigs, is a prime bird-watching area. The Caribbean Sea and Atlantic Ocean, which surround the island, teem with marine life. There over 900 species — including swordfish, lobster and squid— and 400 kinds of mollusks. The country also has one of the world's most important coral barriers — a diver's paradise.

# Cuba's Colorful History

Before the Spanish set foot on the island of Cuba, three Indian tribes inhabited different parts of the country. The Siboneys in the east, the Guanahatabey in the west and the Tainos in the central region. The two Arawak groups—the Siboneys and Tainos—lived in relative peace before the Spanish arrived.

There is no record of the language the Indians spoke, but many of their words were introduced into the Spanish language. The word "Cuba" is thought to have come from the Taino word for 'center of the island'. *Hamaca* (hammock), *tabaco* (tobacco), *cigarro* (cigar), *huracán* (hurrican), *canoa* (canoe) and barbecue are all words of Indian origin.

On October 27, 1492, Columbus discovered Cuba. However, it was not until almost 20 years later, in 1510 that the King of Spain sent Diego Velázquez, to claim Cuba for Spain. The Spanish in their quest for gold and riches decimated the Indian population. Those who were not slaughtered by the Spanish or didn't die from the diseases introduced by the Europeans, were forced into slave labor and worked to death. By 1620, as a result of the Spanish conquest, nearly all of the Indians had been wiped out.

In 1514 Havana was founded. The Spanish soon realized this city's strategic importance. The city was heavily fortified to protect against the incursions of pirates, who raided the island quite frequently and preyed on the treasure laden ships. All the booty and gold from the New World was sent to Spain via Havana. In the meantime, sugar and tobacco were first cultivated commercially. These two crops eventually became a great source of wealth for the country.

The 17th century was a time of growth in Cuba, despite incessant attacks by pirates. Piracy continued to be a problem until the second half of the eighteenth century, when it became more difficult for pirates to make a living because gold was being depleted in Mexico, Central and South America, and convoys and cities had become well protected.

During the 18th century Havana was briefly occupied by the English. Towards the end of the century the English introduced slaves from Africa for sugar plantation work. Cuba's economy grew at this time because of increased sugar and tobacco production.

As a result of the wars for independence that swept Latin America, Spain lost most of its colonies during the first two decades of the 19th century. By 1824 Cuba and Puerto Rico were Spain's only remaining colonies in the New World.

Around the middle of the century, general Narcisco López and Carlos Manuel de Céspedes both led ill-fated attempts to secure Cuba's independence. In 1895 José Martí organized a new rebellion, but was killed. Despite having interest in Cuba, the U.S. remained neutral in the Spanish-Cuban War. However, when an American battleship, the *Maine,* was mysteriously sunk in Havana Bay, the U.S. government decided to intervene.

The Spanish-American War only lasted a few months. On August 2, 1898, Spain relinquished sovereignty over Cuba, and the U.S. 's long role of involvement in Cuba's affairs began. In

1902 a Cuban republic was established, with the U.S. reserving the right of intervention in Cuba in accordance with the terms of the Platt Amendment. This agreement also established the U.S. naval base at Guantánamo Bay.

A series of rulers followed, their regimes plagued by corruption and tumultuous politics. From 1925-1933 Gerardo Machado, who was supported by the U.S., ruled Cuba as a dictator with an iron fist. Discontent grew and Machado's downfall was brought about by Fulgencio Batista in 1933.

Batista soon became as corrupt as his predecessors. Under his rule the wealth was concentrated in very few hands with the rich controlling all of the positions of power. The majority of the people lived in poverty. After ruling until 1944, Batista was defeated in an election and went to Florida. In 1952 he returned to stage a successful coup, suspended the constitution and established a dictatorship. During his reign, Cuba become the playground of the Americans, moral decadence was rampant and many businesses were Mafia-run.

The mob first established a foothold in Cuba during the Prohibition years. During this time the country had the dubious distinction of being the prostitution capital of the Western hemisphere. Cuba also became known as the "Las Vegas" of the Caribbean. Against this background, lawlessness and corruption flourished. Soon many Cuban people became increasingly fed up with corruption and opulence on one side and poverty and injustice on the other side. People began to feel despair under Batista's harsh dictatorship and the seeds of rebellion began to grow.

On July 26th, 1953, a band of young men led by Fidel Castro unsuccessfully attacked the Moncada barracks in Santiago. This event was considered the beginning of the Cuban Revolution. After a long fight, Castro's guerrilla force triumphed and Batista fled the country on January 1, 1959.

The revolutionary government moved towards a state-controlled system. Education was given the highest priority. Today Cuba boasts the highest literacy rate in Latin America— around 95%. Before the revolution, the U.S. virtually controlled Cuba's economy. Castro quickly nationalized all American businesses. Medical care became free and accessible to all the people.

After 1960 Cuba became less dependent on the U.S. and established strong ties with the Soviet Union. This led to a deterioration of relations with the U.S. and the eventual embargo on trade with Cuba which is still in effect today.

The collapse of communism in the Soviet Union and Eastern Europe proved devastating for Cuba's economy. The country lost most of its subsidies and main trading partners. This coupled with other economic problems led to severe shortages, disruption of the food supply and other hardships. The government took desperate measures like legalizing dollars and promoting tourism by establishing joint ventures with Canada and such European countries as Spain.

Despite the above measures, the U.S. embargo still remained in force, economic hardships continued and, in 1994 many Cubans, *los balseros* as the rafters were called, tried to flee the country by raft. Out of desperation there was a reappearance of such capitalistic vices as prostitution. The government had no other choice but to introduce such economic reforms as foreign ownership of businesses and private enterprise.

However, disparity also began to manifest itself between the "haves and have nots" or those earning dollars and those who didn't. Defections also increased during this period as dissatisfaction grew. Many of Cuba's elite, such as pro athletes seeking lucrative contracts, musicians in search of more freedom and artistic expression, doctors and even a couple of Cuban air force pilots, left the island. Although defection was made more difficult, many Cubans continue to try to flee. The most recent defection of note was a group of Cuban baseball stars. They were granted asylum in Costa Rica and eventually ended up playing major league baseball in the U.S.

The Pope's visit to Cuba in early 1998 would prove to be the first sign of a normalization of relations between the U.S. and Cuba. The death of the long-time leader of Miami's Cuban exile community two month's before the Pope's visit and a new generation of younger less confrontational Cuba Americans might eventually help to soften the U.S.'s hard-line stance against Cuba. This should eventually spell the end of the embargo. In addition, the CIA released a report in 1998 stating Cuba no longer posed a threat to the United States.

At one time it was rumored that President Clinton would seek to have Congress lift the embargo against Cuba since he was a lame duck president and really had nothing to lose. Sadly his administration was plagued by so many scandals that he couldn't have lifted the embargo even if he had tried.

In early January of 1999 President Clinton relaxed the sanctions against Cuba. Many experts interpreted this move as the first step to totally lifting the embargo. For the first time since the embargo was established 37 years ago, Washington allowed the sale of food and agriculture supplies to non-government entities and expanded cash transfers, thus increasing the number of Americans permitted to send money to their Cuban relatives. The number of direct charter flights from the U.S. was also increased and direct mail service was reestablished between the U.S. and Cuba.

Finally, there have been both cultural and sports exchanges between the two countries. The president authorized the board of directors of the professional baseball leagues to schedule exhibition games between the Baltimore Orioles and a Cuban all-star team. Some people compare this "baseball diplomacy" to Nixon's "ping-pong diplomacy" which eventually helped normalize relations between the U.S. and China.

# The People

Cuba's nearly 12 million people are mostly Spanish and Africans who came to the island over the past 500 years. About 60% of Cubans consider themselves as white or descendants of Spanish colonial settlers and other immigrants. Around 10% of the population is black, 20% mulatto (a mixture of European and African) and 1% Chinese who were brought in as laborers in the mid-1800s as the slave trade from Africa disappeared. Most of the country's Chinese population lives in Havana's Chinatown.

Cuba's Indian population was virtually wiped out centuries ago, so the Spanish imported 800,000 African slaves. The percentage of blacks is much higher in eastern Cuba. These figures may not be accurate since Cuba is a 'melting pot'. The races have so intermingled that it is impossible to classify Cuba's population mixtures with total accuracy.

Cubans seem to prefer the urban lifestyle. Nearly 70% live in cities and towns with a third living in Havana province and a fifth in the city of Havana itself — around 2.2 million. Santiago has around 440,000 inhabitants, Camaguey 300,000, Holguín 240,000, Guantánamo 208,000, and Santa Clara 200,000. Other areas in descending order of inhabitants are Bayamo, Cienfuegos, Pinar del Río, Las Tunas, Matanzas, Manzanillo, Ciego de Avila and Sanctí Spíritus.

All of Cuba's people brought with them their traditions and culture, so present Cuban traditions, music, dance and religion show aspects of the different groups.

Most Cubans are Roman Catholics. There are also a small number of Protestants and a Jewish community of several thousand in Havana who still express a sense of community despite their dwindling numbers. Prior to the revolution there were around 20,000 Jews in Cuba, most of whom sought refuge during World War II. There is still a Kosher butcher shop, a synagogue and a Hebrew Sunday School for children in Havana.

Many of Cuba's blacks are followers of various Afro-Cuban cults or religions similar to the voodoo cult of Haiti. These cults have their origins in Africa, were introduced by African slaves and are a blend of elements from Catholicism and African native traditions. They are reflected in the country's literature, poetry, dance songs and dramatic arts. Santería is the most widespread of the Afro-Cuban religions.

One thing that sets Cubans apart from other Caribbean peoples is their work ethic. Of all Latin American people Cubans are by far the hardest working and are known for their business acumen and entrepreneurial skills. However, the Cuban people are unique in that they combine a strong work ethic with the ability to enjoy themselves like other Latins.

As in most Latin American countries the family is the center of most Cuban's lives. Family ties are strong and much time is spent with one's family. Since the revolution women have made great strides. Now they compose almost half of the work force with many standing out in such fields as law and medicine. Furthermore, husbands are expected to do their share of household duties.

Despite all of these advancements towards sexual equality, Cuba is still a male dominated society. Women have made great progress in the workplace, but some are still often relegated to doing most household tasks. This is probably due to the deep-rooted institution of machismo found in all Latin American countries. In case you don't know, *machismo* is the belief in the natural superiority of men in all fields of endeavor. It becomes the obsession and constant preoccupation of many Latin men to demonstrate they are *macho* in a variety of ways.

There is no telling what lengths men will go to in order to demonstrate their virility. A man's virility is measured by the

# Damn Yankees!

## By Jay Trettein

As a bartender at a large hotel in San José, Costa Rica, I meet many tourists and business people who visit Cuba. They either love the country or hate it. I'm one of those people who can't wait to return.

If you fly on the inexpensive Cuban airline, CUBANA, get ready for delays and a bumpy ride. But customs in and out of Cuba is effortless. True for any country you've never visited, but with Cuba it's especially correct, get advice from someone who has been there. Havana is a big city. Learn about the cab system. At first negotiating with the many independent drivers who approach you seems a bargain but I feel using the governmentally regulated PANATAXI turns out to be the best value. Hint: If you're on a long trip, let the driver know you don't mind if the meter is turned off. He'll make money and you'll save money.

Hotel prices are comparable to anywhere in the Caribbean but most tourists opt for the private homes that provide accommodations. Choose a neighborhood you like, walk around looking like a tourist and someone will suggest a place to stay. I found a room easily for $25 a night with a/c, my own keys, private bath, access to a salon with tv and a balcony. Food in restaurants... so-so. Nightlife...late-late, and too late for me. And if Hemmingway slept and drank at all the places that tout his name...he must have been the most rested alcoholic in history.

All of the Cubans were very friendly and helpful. I met an old Cuban man in the Central Park one morning across from the Hotel Inglaterra. Together with a cab driver friend of his they went out of their way to show me all of the sights and watering holes in Havana.

The United States embargo of the beautiful, vivacious Cuban people is one of the most stupid diplomatic mistakes in modern times and should end.

There is virtually little or no street crime in Cuba. My biggest problem...I had bought a New York Yankee cap with me anticipating the Yankees World Series. The cap always provoked conversation as Orlando Hernández, "El Duque", winner of game #2 in the Yankee's sweep had just recently fled Cuba on a raft. While walking along the sidewalk, a teenager on a bicycle grabbed my cap. Kid's prank, and if he'd asked me for it , I would have probably given it to him. Socialism...I guess!

number of seductions or *conquistas* he makes, or his capacity to consume alcohol. Women walking alone on the street are the target of sexual comments and innuendoes by men. These *piropos* or flirtatious remarks range from ordinary compliments about a woman's beauty to obscene and often insulting phrases. Among males virility is highly esteemed and disparaging names are pinned on homosexuals.

The greatest successes of the revolution are in the fields of education and public health. About 40% of Cuba's budget is currently devoted to education and public health. As we mentioned, Cubans are well-educated people. Education is compulsory up to the 12th grade and is free at all levels from pre-school to university . Cubans enjoy learning. About a third of the people attend some type of classes regularly. Cuba's literacy speaks for itself. Before the revolution only about 75% of the people could read or write with 25% being semiliterate. Today most of the people are literate, with illiteracy almost being eliminated. This accomplishment alone speaks for Cuba's outstanding educational system. The country now boasts around one teacher for every forty inhabitants. There are also 60 universities located all around the country.

Despite the hardships of the U.S. embargo Cubans are relatively well-off when compared people at the lower end of the economic spectrum in other Latin American countries. Because of this Cubans are considered to be "The richest poor people in the world."

Cubans are a healthy people with a life expectancy of 75— one of the highest in Latin America and as high as many developed countries. The country also has the lowest infant mortality rate in Latin America. There is approximately 1 doctor for  very 400 people. In the year 2000 the World Health Organization ranked Cuba's public health system as the 39th best of almost 200 systems worldwide.

Cubans are generally gregarious, happy, hospitable, like foreigners, outgoing, vivacious and have a great sense of humor. Their many *cubanismos,* or witty expressions, and piropos reflect their sense of humor. If you are lucky enough to understand Spanish you can really enjoy listening to Cubans interact with each other.

Cuba's vibrant culture is most typified by their music. Perhaps in no other field have Cubans excelled more than music. They love to dance and play music ranging from tropical to jazz. Most of Cuba's rich musical heritage comes from its black population. Afro-Cuban is a mixture of Spanish and African music. The *rumba, son, salsa, guajira mambo, cha- cha-cha* and *conga* are all songs and dances native to Cuba. All have enjoyed international popularity at one time or another. There are even special instruments of Cuban origin invented to play this Afro-Cuban music, such as the maracas.

Cubans love to party and dancing is an integral part of most Cuban's lives. Sensual music and dance are their preferred pleasures. Music seems to fill the air wherever you are in Cuba and it seems someone is always playing music or dancing. Almost every celebration, private or public, includes some type of dancing. People can be seen dancing at carnivals, fiestas and in local dance halls.

Cubans in general are fun-loving despite the economic hardships they have had to endure in recent times. Cuba is a sexually permissive society. Sex seems to be the favorite hobby of many Cubans. Promiscuity is widespread as are extramarital affairs. Sensuality seems to pervade the air and is reflected in the country's music and inviting piropos. Because most of the people have to share homes and apartments, privacy is rare. So, love hotels— special places where people go to make love—are flourishing. A Cuban friend once told us, "The reason we enjoy sex so much is because it is one of the few things we can do for free here."

Besides music and dance Cubans enjoy sports which play an important role in their lives. Cuba's favorite sport is baseball. Cubans are fanatical when it comes to this sport. Even after the revolution it has still remained popular. Many big league players have come from Cuba. Cubans have also distinguished themselves as world-class athletes in boxing, track and field and Olympic competition.

If you want an graphic picture of modern Cuba's people and culture, read Tom Miller's insightful book, Trading With the Enemy.

# (HAPTER 3

## EXPLORING (UBA

### Some Things to (onsider

The best way to decide where you will want to settle in Cuba, is to visit those areas having activities that fit your particular lifestyle. Consider the things you like to do and then check out the towns, beaches or cities which best suit your needs and interests.

If you are accustomed to living in an urban area offering a variety of cultural events, entertainment and other stimulating activities, then small towns or rural living is not for you. You can eliminate living in a city if you are the type of person who is easily annoyed by traffic, noise, pollution and other inconveniences usually associated with urban living. One advantage to living in a rural area or small town is that the cost of living is lower.

Residing at an isolated resort may seem attractive, but there is a downside. Beach properties are usually an excellent investment but prices can be high due to demand. Also, most of the population is seasonal and you may find it difficult to

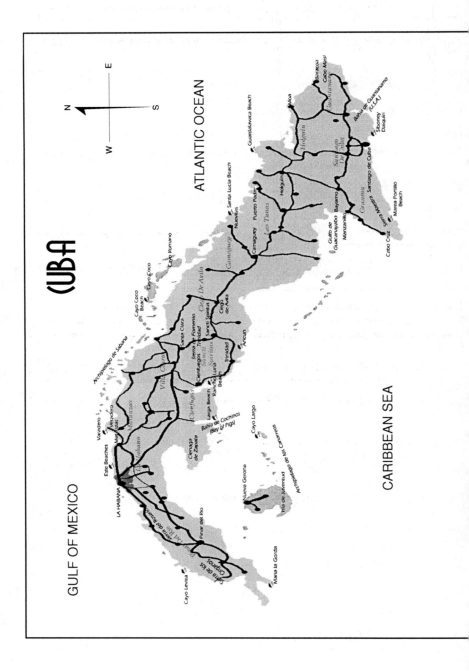

making long-term relationships. In non-resort areas the population fluctuates less thus making it easier for enduring friendships. The "off season" can be dull and boring for some people. However, there are some people who relish the peace and quiet.

Another factor in making your choice is weather. In the tropics the low lands are hot and higher elevations and mountains areas are cooler: the higher you get the lower the temperature and the lower you go the hotter it gets. Living at the beach is nice for a while but can get old when one grows tired of the insects and humidity. Isolated beaches can pose problems when it comes to emergency medical care. So, look for the climate that best agrees with you.

# (uba from Tip to Tip

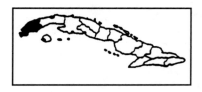

The province of **Pinar del Río** is Cuba's third largest and located on the western tip of the island. It is known for its natural beauty, dramatic landscapes, incredible scenery and for producing some of the best tobacco and cigars in the world. Pinar del Río is considered by many to be the most beautiful province in Cuba. The small city of **Pinar del Río** (125,000), about 110 miles west of Havana, is the most important town in the province with the same name. It is named for the many pine trees found in the area when the city was originally founded. The city has many neo-classical buildings and other architecture. A bank, bookstore, library and museum are also found in this city.

Located in a valley with the same name, the beautiful town of Viñales is a national monument. It is a photographer's paradise. A unique string of limestone buttes called mogotes are a prominent feature of this area. There are also many nearby caves worth exploring. The best known is the **Indian Cave** which may actually be explored by taking a boat ride through underground caverns. You can also do rock climbing, hiking, and horseback riding and there are two mineral water spas, **San Vicente** and **San Diego de los Baños**. The latter is about 90 miles southwest of Havana. Noted for its scenic beauty, **Soroa** in the *Sierra de Rosario* Mountains, 60 miles from Havana, is a botanical resort and nature lover's dream come true. The 700 varieties of orchids found in the garden have to be seen to believed. There are some 35,000 square kilometers devoted solely to orchids. A *mirador* or lookout and impressive waterfall are found nearby. While there, you can stay at the hotel and dine at the *Castillo de las Nubes* (the Castle of the Clouds) located on the highest peak in the area. The panoramic view is unparalleled. The beaches found in this province are less accessible and less developed than those found in other areas. **Cayo Levisa** is on a small key off the north coast of this province. By far the best beaches in the province are found here. There are some offshore reefs and the diving is excellent. **Playa María la Gorda** is a nice beach in *Bahía de Corrientes* at the extreme southwest tip.

The **Island of the Youth** or *Isla de la Juventud*, known originally as the Island of the Pines before the revolution, lies about 30 miles off the south coast of Cuba, at the mouth of the Gulf of Batabanó. It is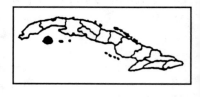
the largest of Cuba's offshore islands. It is said to be the place Robert Louis Stevenson had in mind when he wrote *Treasure Island*, because, allegedly, there is a pirate treasure buried there. The island has plenty of virgin beaches you can explore. The many off shore ship wrecks, underwater caves, coral reefs, abundance of marine life and crystal clear water offer some of the best diving in the Caribbean, especially between Point Francés and Point Pedernales. *Punta de Este* has a beautiful beach and caves nearby. *Nueva Gerona* is the island's largest town.

About 75 miles east of The Island of the Youth lies the resort **Cayo Largo**. This 16 mile-long island is a place you go to "get away from it all." The endless white sand beaches and crystal-clear water make it a good place to relax and participate in a number of water sports like horseback riding, snorkeling, fishing, sailing, diving and windsurfing . This spot is popular with vacationing Europeans. If you are a person who likes this type of laid back resort atmosphere and beach lifestyle, either of the latter two resorts would be suitable for you.

Almost a quarter of Cuba's 10 million people live in **Havana** or *La Habana* —Cuba's capital city in the province with the same name. It lies about 90 miles south of Key West, Florida. It is the largest city in the Caribbean and one of the oldest in the Americas. Politically and culturally, Havana is the most important city in the country. It is situated at the mouth of a deep bay and natural harbor. Before the revolution Havana was considered the most beautiful and impressive city in the Caribbean.

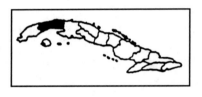

Despite being run-down, it is still a fascinating city and has some of the best 16th century Spanish colonial architecture in the world.  As you will see in the section on entertainment, there is a wide range of activities in and around the Havana area— plenty to do to keep busy: restaurants, bars, movies, night clubs, parks, a wealth of historic museums and so much more.

Havana covers about 290 square miles and is divided into 15 districts or municipalities. Some are on the ocean and others far from the center of the city.  It is easy to get lost or confused because many of the city's main avenues have two names. Be aware that the residents use the old, pre-revolution names. Addresses are usually given as locations with street numbers being used once in a while. Most of Havana is laid out on a grid pattern like other Cuban cities.

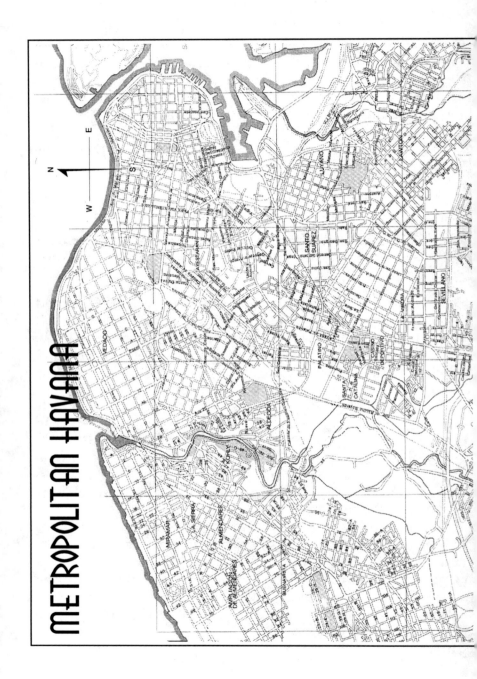

METROPOLITAN HAVANA

# DOWNTOWN HAVANA

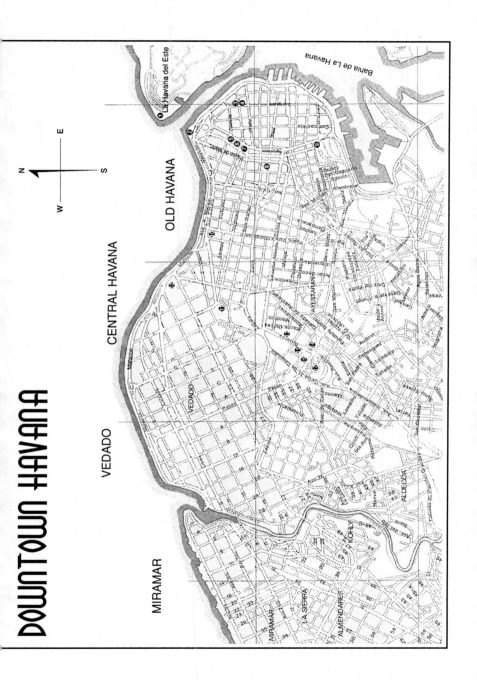

MIRAMAR

VEDADO

CENTRAL HAVANA

OLD HAVANA

Bahía de La Havana

La Havana del Este

Malecón

AYESTARAN

MIRAMAR

LA SIERRA

ALMENDARES

KOHLY

ALDECOA

The center of the city is divided into several sections, three of which are the most interesting. **Havana Vieja** or Old Havana, is a diamond shaped area in the historical heart of the city. It remains a monument to the past with its narrow cobblestone streets, old aristocratic mansions, plazas and magnificent buildings. In Havana Vieja a total of 1,853 buildings of different styles can be found, constructed during five centuries: 144 belong to the XVI and XVII, 200 to the XVIII, 463 to the XIX and 902 to the XX.

For over 350 years it was the entire city. This part of the city is laid out on a grid pattern in the typical Spanish colonial style and has some fine examples of colonial architecture. It is located at the west side of the entrance to the harbor and has its center on the shore of Havana Bay. There are also numerous hotels, museums, bars and restaurants in this area which overflow with Cuban rhythm and flavor. The best way to explore this area is on foot since there is so much to see.

On the sea-side end is the *Malecón* or seashore promenade sometimes called *Avenida Maceo*. It runs for three miles along the coast from the *Castillo de la Punta* at the north end of *Havana* Vieja to the Almendares River at the west end of Vedado district continuing through the Miramar District and eventually becoming the highway to Mariel.

It is the most scenic area in the city and dotted with seaside restaurants, bars, monuments, office buildings, parks and tall hotels. The Malecón is a great place for a strolling and viewing breathtaking sunsets or just sitting on the seawall watching the locals sunbathe, swim, fish off the rocks or flirt with the many attractive women who pass-by. During the day it is the gathering place for families, young lovers and *jineteros* (street hustlers).

**Central Havana**, or 'Centro', is laid out in a near perfect grid in the area between the *Paseo del Prado* to the east and the neighborhood of Vedado to the west. This area is considered to be the heart of the city. The *Malecón* runs along the north boundary of this district. There architecture in this area is very impressive. *El Capitolio* or the capitol building, is modeled after the Capitol in Washington, D.C. It was inaugurated in 1929 and today is a museum, convention and exposition center. There is a small Chinatown, but nothing like the ones in San Francisco, New York or Los Angeles. The remnants of Cuba's once thriving Chinese community live in this part of the city.

**Vedado**, to the west, is Havana's main commercial and residential center. There are mostly hotels and apartments located in this part of the city. There are some art deco buildings like the ones found in Miami. The University of Havana, and a couple of museums are among the attractions found there.

**La Rampa**, the name for Calle 23 from Calle L to the sea in Vedado, is the the five block area and the vibrant nerve center of Havana. It begins at around the halfway point on the Malecón and ends at the *Havana Libre Hotel*. The *Hotel Capri*, *Hotel Riviera* and *Hotel Nacional* are high rise hotels which originally catered to Americans in the pre-Castro days. Travel agencies, restaurants, cabarets, stores and theaters are found within this district. One of the cities most popular meeting places is the famous Coppelia Ice Cream Parlor and Park.

The exclusive suburb of **Miramar**, west of *Vedado* on the west bank of the Almendares River, gives us a glimpse of life before the revolution with its tree-lined avenues, mansions and villas. This is where the richest of Havana's residents lived before the revolution. Now, most of the mansions are embassies, offices and schools. The main drag of this formerly glitzy upper class area is appropriately called Fifth Avenue. The *Acuario Nacional* or National Aquarium (Avenida 1 No 6002 at calle 60) is found in this neighborhood. It contains saltwater fish and performing dolphins. The Convention Center and Tropicana Nightclub are also found here along with a few good restaurants.

To the west of Miramar are a string of seemingly endless suburbs. On Havana's outskirts there are many places of interest.

About eight miles west of Havana on the coast is the **Hemingway Marina**. It is Cuba's largest marina and has space for over 400 yachts. There are restaurants — including the famous **Papas**, a hotel, supermarket and shopping center in this complex. The marina is the site of the annual Ernest Hemingway Fishing Tournament held each May. Scuba diving, water skiing and jet skiing are also available at the marina.

About 7 miles east of Havana is the suburb and little town of **San Francisco de Paula**, where the *Museo Hemingway* or Hemingway Museum, is found. It contains many of the late writer's relics. **Cojímar**, about 6 miles east of Havana, is a picturesque little fishing village famous for being the setting of Hemingway's classic novel, *The Old Man and the Sea*. This village has a laid-back Caribbean atmosphere and a seafront promenade. Go to **La Terraza** restaurant to check out the Hemingway memorabilia. It was a favorite local hangout of his, and the sea food is delicious.

**Playas del Este**, Havana's eastern beaches, offer something for beach lovers. There are a series of fourteen beaches strung along miles of beautiful coastline. **Bacuranao** is the first beach east of Havana. **Santa María del Mar** is the longest of these beaches and is as popular with tourists as is Guanabo with the locals. Other good beaches are **Mégano** and **Boca Ciega**. The last of these beaches **Jibacoa**, about fifty miles east of Havana, is a good snorkeling beach because of the numerous reefs offshore. It is less expensive than most of the other resorts in the area. All these beaches have accommodations and food as well as fine white sand, crystal clear blue water and recreational facilities. These nearby beaches can be reached by either bus or electric train.

If readers wish to know more about Havana they should read Christopher Baker's *Havana Handbook*. This fine work is the companion guide to Mr. Baker's classic, *Cuba Handbook*. It is the first ever travel guidebook in English devoted solely to the Cuba capital and is filled with 450 pages of indispensable information. Please see the "Suggested Reading " section in Chapter 9 for additional details.

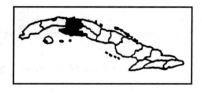

**Matanzas**, which means 'slaughter' or massacre in Spanish, is the main city in Cuba's second largest province bearing the same name. Located on Matanzas Bay, it lies about 65 miles east of Havana and 21 miles west of Varadero. The city has a population of around 100,000. It is a port and used to be the center of Cuba's sugar industry. Today it is an industrial town. In the 19th century, Matanzas was nicknamed the Athens of Cuba and was the home of many well-known intellectuals. In recent times this city has taken a back seat to the resort of Varadero. Life is slower-paced and more laid-back than Havana. There are a few good museums, restaurants and night spots in this city. The famous **Bellamar Caves**, five miles south of the city, are Cuba's oldest tourist sight and are considered a popular attraction. These caves are about 2,500 meters long and have a stream inside.

Birdwatchers and nature lovers will enjoy the **Zapata Peninsula** located about 100 miles from Havana in the southern part of Matanzas province. It is the largest wetlands in the Caribbean, boasting a bird sanctuary and is a virtual bird watcher's paradise. In addition 200 species of birds, turtles, alligators, fish, mammals and other forms of wildlife abound. This area was named for its shape that resembles the outline of a shoe (*zapato* in Spanish).

However, the main attraction of Matanzas Province is **Varadero**, Cuba's most famous beach resort. It has become the tourist capital of Cuba and the largest tourist complex in the Caribbean. *Varadero* is to Cuba what Cancún is to Mexico.

Located three hours by car from Havana, its beaches are some of the finest in the Caribbean, if not the world. They are a sight to behold. The resort is found on the Hicacos Peninsula and has 12 miles of uninterrupted white-sand beaches bordered by shallow, clear turquoise waters.

**Varadero's** unparalleled beauty has attracted tourists for almost a century. Originally a playground for wealthy Americans, it has now become popular with Canadians and European sun worshipers.

There are a number of modern hotels in the area. Golf lovers will enjoy the 18 -hole course, *Club de Golf las Americas*, at the beautiful Du Pont Estate. The nightlife, discos, movie theaters, cabarets, restaurants, fastfood cafes serving everything from pizzas to hamburgers, satellite TV showing HBO and MTV, numerous bars and other entertainment will keep you from getting bored. Discoteca La Bamba, Cabaret Continental and Palacio de la Rumba are all famous for their nightlife.Of course, there are a variety of watersports, including scuba diving, and many excursions to keep you busy. The town of Varadero is located nearby.

**Playa Larga** and **Playa Girón** are other excellent beaches found in Matanzas Province. This area is famous for scuba diving. Near Playa Girón is the *Bahía de los Cochinos* (Bay of Pigs), the sight of the ill-fated invasion attempt by Cuban exiles in 1961. The **Laguna del Tesoro** is a lake famous for its freshwater fishing and largemouth bass.

**Cienfuegos** is Cuba's smallest province. It is surrounded by the provinces of Matanzas to the west, Villa Clarita to the north, Sancti Spíritus to the east and the Caribbean to the south. On Cuba's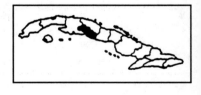
south coast lies the city of Cienfuegos, the capital of Cienfuegos province. Its name means'100 fires' but is really named for *José Cienfuegos*, the one-time Captain General of Cuba. Situated on the north shore of Jagua Bay—the city's main feature— this city

is the chief town of its province and one of Cuba's important seaports. This pleasant seaside city is known as the "Pearl of the South" and has a slight cosmopolitan feeling. It is laid out on a rectangular grid. Like Havana, the city has a Malecón, or seaside promenade, facing the ocean.

Thirty miles to the south of Cienfuegos is **Playa Rancho Luna** which has facilities for every type of beach activity. There is also a string of other good beaches like **Playitas**. Fishermen will be happy to know there are a few large lakes in this province. There are also caves to explore and a hot springs.

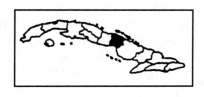

The city of **Ciego de Avila** is between the cities of *Santa Clara* and *Camaguey* in a province with the same name. There is not much to see in this city, but the surrounding area is worth exploring. **Laguna de Leche** and **Laguna Redonda** are two well-known lakes in the region.

**Cayo Coco** is the main tourist island off the coast of this province. It has white sand beaches and is connected to the mainland by an 18-mile long causeway. The smaller **Cayo Guillermo** key, just west of **Cayo Coco** is connected to the latter by a causeway. It was one of Hemingway's favorite fishing spots and stomping grounds.

The city of **Santa Clara** (200,000) is located 171 miles from Havana and 195 miles from *Varadero* along the Central Highway. It is a pleasant university city in the middle of the island and is the capital of Villa Clara Province. There is not much to see in the way of architecture but there are a few good museums. One of the last battles of the revolution was fought in this city before Castro entered Havana. About 30 miles from the city of Santa Clara is **Lake Habanilla**,

Cuba's best fishing lake which is also noted for its largemouth bass. A number of mountain and beach areas are worth exploring in this province.

About 50 miles from **Cienfuegos** in Central Cuba and south of *Santa Clara* in *Sancti Spíritus* Province, lies **Trinidad** — a beautifully preserved colonial city of about 50,000 inhabitants and Cuba's third oldest settlement. It is considered a national monument with its cobblestone streets and roofs of ancient red tiles. There are several good museums in this lovely town. **Ancón**, about 7 miles from Trinidad, has a coral reef offshore, good fishing and scuba diving, and is one of the country's prettiest beaches. **Costa Sur** is another nearby beach resort to visit. The health resort town of Topes de Collantes in the Sierra del Escambray mountains is worth visiting.

**Sancti Spíritus** (80,000) is the next town of importance found in a province with the same name. Located east of Trinidad and in the center of the country it is one of Cuba's original towns. This city  would not be a good place to live because it is rather unattractive and lacks infrastructure. Therefore, most tourists bypass this town. Just outside the city is **Lake Zaza**, another lake famous for its largemouth bass.

**Camagüey** is Cuba's largest, but most sparsely populated, province. The city of Camagüey is Cuba's third largest city with a population of 250,000. It is the most important city in the province and Cuba's  biggest inland city. Like the majority of Cuba's important cities and towns, it is located along the Central Highway or *Carretera Central*. Despite not having a seaport it has its particular beauty, culture and charm. It is considered a national monument and there are many sights to see. The old colonial section has a typical irregular layout and elegant Spanish style architecture predominates.

There is good fishing at nearby at **Presa La Manana** de **Santa Ana** and **Presa Muñoz Lakes**. A number of excellent beaches are only a few hours by car from the city. The province's main tourist attraction is the resort of **Playa Santa Lucía**, about 65 miles north east and a two-hour drive . It is one the country's most outstanding beaches. It boasts a beautiful 10 mile long beach protected by a coral reef. Needless to say, the diving, swimming and snorkeling are great.

**Playa Coco** —considered by many as Cuba's most beautiful beach— and **Cayo Sabinal**, a huge key with terrific beaches, are some of the other points of interest in this part of the country.

**Las Tunas** is the capital city of the province with the same name. It is basically a center for sugar and rice growing and cattle raising. So the city is of little interest to the average tourist. It is not surprising, 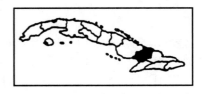 therefore, that most visitors choose to pass through or bypass this city all together.

The cozy city has a couple of buildings of historical interest and parks to see. Like most small cities and towns, there is a post office, hospital and other basic services. There are also a train and bus terminals found here. However, if you are adventurous there are a couple of beaches worth visiting. The best are: **Playa Covarrubias, Playa Uvero** and **Playa Herradura**.

**Holguín**, (225,000) in the eastern part of the country, is the most important town in its province and Cuba's fourth largest city. The city is famous for its historical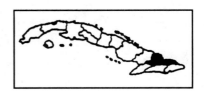

importance. There are museums, monuments and other historical sites in the downtown area.

On the Atlantic coast the resort of **Guardavaca** (meaning 'watch the cow' in Spanish)—about 40 miles north east of Holguín, is one of Cuba's best white sand beaches and considered by many to be the second resort after Varadero. The water is clear blue and the resort is surrounded by coconut palms and other tropical vegetation. There is an off-shore coral reef for diving or snorkeling.

Nearby **Playa Don Lino** to the west is less developed, but has a gorgeous white sand beach and two coral reefs. **Ciego Estero** and **Bahía Naranja** are other beaches to the west of Guardavava.

**Bayamo** (130,000), the capital of **Granma Province**, was the second town founded by the Spanish in Cuba. It has played an important role in Cuba's history. It is the place Manuel Céspedes declared  independence from Spain. The town has become a tourist attraction and there is plenty to see in the town itself and surrounding area.

To the southwest are Cuba's most impressive mountains, The Sierra Maestra. These Mountains dominate the province and offer hiking and hunting, and fishing at **Virama** and **Leonero Lakes**. *Gran Parque Nacional Sierra Madre* was Castro's base of operations during the Cuban Revolution.

Thirty-seven miles west of Baymo, in the Gulf of Guacanayabo, lies the port city of **Manzanillo**, Granma's second largest city and a fishing port. The best beaches in the area are: **Playa de las Coloradas** (on the southwest coast), **Playa Carenero** and **Marea del Portillo** on the south coast.

**Santiago de Cuba** province is nestled between Granma, Holguín and Guantanamo provinces in the heart of the Sierra Madre mountain range. Cuba's second largest city is **Santiago de Cuba** on the south-east coast near the eastern tip of the island in a sheltered bay at the foothills of the Sierra Maestra Mountains. Like most large Cuban cities it is the capital of its province with the same name. It is known as "the cradle of the revolution" because of the revolutionary activities that have taken place there. Santiago is also the most Caribbean and charmingly picturesque city in Cuba—which is reflected in the relaxed life-style of its people and tropical ambiance. Santiago is a hilly city with colonial architecture and a fortress. The best way to see the city is on foot.

After Havana, Santiago has the most culture and is Cuba's most exotic and ethnically diverse city. The Afro-Cuban tradition is very strong in this city as reflected by the music and the annual carnival—considered Cuba's best. The nightlife isn't as good as in Havana, but is a close second. There is a lot to see and do in and around the city including discos and restaurants. Cabaret music is plentiful and there are many spots to hear Latin music.

On the outskirts of Santiago is **Baconao Park**. It is the largest park in Cuba and has a long series of beaches with hotels and restaurants. To the east of Santiago is the Gran Piedra (Big Stone)—a giant outcropping from which you can see Jamaica or the Dominican Republic on a clear day. There are a series of good beaches east of the city. **Siboney** is the closest beach and popular with the locals. **Juragua** and **Daiquirí** (in Bacanao Park) and a dozen other well known beaches are found in this province. **Balneario de Sol**, about 50 minutes drive from Santiago, is a beautiful resort.

**Guantánamo**, 70 miles from Santiago on the south-east coast, is the chief town in Guantánamo Province. It is near the famous U.S. base with the same name. One of Cuba's most famous songs, *"Guanatanamera"* was named for this city. The town is rather drab and doesn't have a lot to offer. **Yateritas** and **Playitas** are two of the most visited beaches in this province.

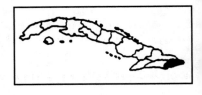

Beyond Guanatánamo lies the **Baracoa**—Cuba's oldest town and first capital of the country. There are a couple of interesting forts and other buildings dating from the colonial era. This town is off-the-beaten-track but definitely worth visiting.

Since Cuba is such an large island, it is virtually impossible to give detailed descriptions of every area in the scope of this book. We recommended you read Christopher Baker's best-selling *Cuba* and *Havana Handbooks* listed in the "Suggested Reading" section of this book. Then go out and explore the island for a suitable place to live taking into consideration your lifestyle and the other factors we discuss through this book.

# CHAPTER 4

## PLACES TO GO AND THINGS TO DO IN CUBA

### Advice for Retirees and Others Living Abroad

Starting a life in a foreign country presents challenges for many people. For the first time they may be confronted with having a plethora of leisure time and the problem of what to do with it. As you will see throughout this chapter, Cuba is a wonderful place to live. In addition there are many interesting activities from which to choose. In Cuba you have no excuse for being bored or inactive, unless you are just plain lazy. There is some hobby or pastime for everyone regardless of age or interest. Even if you can't pursue your favorite hobbies, you can get involved in something new and exciting.

Best of all, by participating in some of the activities in this chapter, you will meet other people with common interests and cultivate new friendships in the process. Initially, most people you meet will also probably be expatriates, so you probably won't need much Spanish to enjoy yourself.

Whatever you do, don't make the mistake of being idle. Use your time constructively and get out and enjoy all Cuba has to offer.

# Cuba's Pristine Beaches

*"He always thought of the sea as 'la mar' which is what people called her in Spanish when they love her. Sometimes those who love her say bad things of her, but they are always said as though she were a woman."*

*- Ernest Hemingway,*
**The Old Man and the Sea**

Cuba is a beach lovers' paradise. There are about three-hundred unspoiled beaches scattered along Cuba's many miles of irregular coastline. Most of these beaches are undeveloped, and considered among the best in the Caribbean, have white sand and are bounded by crystal-clear ocean water. The temperature of the water ranges between 75 and 80 degrees depending on the location of the beach. The Atlantic waters tend to be a few degrees cooler than the Caribbean.

A third of Cuba's beaches are readily accessible and fifty have hotels and other facilities for tourists. As you know from reading the last chapter, **Varadero** on the north coast is the most famous of all Cuban beaches. **Guardavaca** is another popular beach on the Atlantic side of the island. **Santa Lucia** in Camagüey Province is considered a diver's paradise. **Playas del Este** near Havana are the beaches frequented by the majority of Havana's residents, or *havaneros*, on weekends and holidays.

There are also spectacular beaches along the Caribbean coast. Most areas have facilities for sailing, fishing trips, jet skiing, surfing, catamarans, body surfing, windsurfing, parasailing and every imaginable water sport for the adventurous traveller. Near the city of **Santiago de Cuba** many excellent beaches can be found. You can stay in Santiago and visit the beaches in this area.

Cuba's abundance of coral reefs and cays, variety of colorful marine fauna, over 900 species of fish and crystal-clear water make it the perfect place for diving buffs. Cuba is surrounded by one of the world's largest coral reefs. Diving is fantastic and Cuba's number one water sport. The island has over 30 dive sites from which to choose. You don't have to go far from Havana to find diving sites since Jicoba and the surrounding beaches have diving locations.

Cuba is one of the few places where you can actually explore offshore shipwrecks. There are over 1,000 sunken shipwrecks scattered around Cuba's waters. There are sunken Spanish galleons and 50 diving sites including caves found off the coast of the **Island of the Youth** or *La Isla de la Juventud*. Other areas include Playa Santa Lucía, Guardalavaca, Cayo Coco, Playa Ancón, Varadero and Playa Girón to name a few. Most resorts rent equipment, have diving shops and, if you are a novice, you may even take diving lessons. Cuba has certified diving instructors. Check out the diving shop at the Hemingway Marina Tel: (21) 5277. Near Playas del Este be sure to visit the Marina Puertosol scuba center. There is a complete description of Cuba's dive sites at: **www.cubatravel.com/:mx/cuba**.

The waters around Cuba are also perfect for yachting. There are marinas or *fondeaderos* and other facilities in Havana, Varadero and the Island of the Youth. Yachting excursions are also available. Those bringing yachts or other vessels from the U.S. and other countries should check with Cuban customs to find how long a boat may be kept in the country and the paper work involved.

One would need volumes to describe all of Cuba's beaches in detail, so we have provided a map in this guide for your convenience. It doesn't show every beach on the island—only those which can be reached easily.

# An Outdoorsman's Paradise

Fishermen will love Cuba since it is surrounded on all sides by ocean. Cuba's waters have some of the best sportfishing in the world. Although there is a large variety of edible fish near the coast, only a few species are fished for sport. Snook, tarpon, grouper, sailfish and marlin are the most popular game fish. The **Hemingway Marina**, west of Havana, has world class facilities for sportfishing. There are several companies offering sportfishing. The Hemingway International Marlin Fishing Tournament is held there yearly in May or June. There are other deep-sea fishing events and tournaments throughout the year.

Cuba is dotted with numerous man-made lakes for freshwater fishing. The country's lakes teem with largemouth bass—the most popular freshwater fish. **Lake Hanabanilla** in the Escambray Mountain Range is one of the most famous 'fishing holes'. The best inland fishing is found at **Lake Zaza**. **La Redonda Lake, Laguna Grande** in Pinar del Río province and **Tesoro Lake** in Matanzas province are also good fishing areas.

Liberal hunting laws make Cuba ideal for hunters. Pheasant, doves and quail are some of the game birds found in Cuba. Deer, wild pigs, and other mammals may also be hunted. There are about fifteen key hunting reserves located around the island. A number can be reached quite easily from Havana. Most hunting resorts offer lodging, guides, and all types of hunting equipment. INTUR issues seasonal hunting permits.

Because of its hundreds of miles of limestone cave formations, Cuba is one of the best places in the world for cave exploration. Almost every province has caves. The Caves of **Bellamar** or *Las Cuevas de Bellamar*, south of the city of Matanzas, are considered the best in Cuba. These caves are about a mile and a half long with vaulted ceilings and beautifully colored stalagmite and stalactite formations, and under ground streams. North of the small town of Viñales is the **Indian Caves** or *Cuevas de los Indios*. This cave system may be explored on foot or by boat. At the end of the trail visitors can climb in a row boat and follow the underground stream to the cave's end.

Camping and hiking are other activities in which you may participate. There are campgrounds located outside of most towns, by rivers, at beach areas and mountain resorts. Hikers can find trails to explore and breath taking scenery in Cuba's mountain ranges. The Sierra Maestra Mountains and Soroa are excellent places to explore on foot. Nature lovers, bird watchers and botanists will find a lot to see all over this tropical outdoor paradise. Horseback riding is offered at most resort areas.

Golf lovers will find two courses — the 18-hole Havana Golf Club located 10 minutes from downtown and the 18-hole Varadero Golf Club at Varadero. The first has a pro shop, rents high-quality clubs, has caddies, charges a $30 green fee and offers memberships at a reasonable price. The latter, located on the former Dupont summer retreat , has a clubhouse, offers caddys, golfcarts and costs around $60.00 to play all 18 holes. There is little doubt that, in the future, new courses will be constructed as foreign investment helps to improve the country's infrastructure.

A few more golf courses are going to be built in the country in the next couple of years. Canadian and Scottish Companies are involved in a Cuban joint venture to build 18 hole golf courses throughout Cuba to satisfy tourist demands. To keep up with what is going on in the Cuban golf scene see: www.golfcuba.com.

Also check out www.purecubaplay.com to find out about other outdoor activities like horseriding and dude ranches. At www.cubafun.com you may find activities related to: golf, fishing safaris, hunting, natural spas, nature reserves, water-skiing, underground caves and much more.

# What to Do In and Around Havana

The city of **Havana** has a wealth of activities to keep a person busy. If you are the type of person who is accustomed to the stimulation and hustle bustle of urban living to stay occupied, Havana is probably the best place for you to reside. It is a city for walking. If you enjoy seeing the sights on foot you may stroll along the seaside Malecón or admire the colonial architecture like the cathedral. There are many interesting sights around the Plaza de la Revolución. You will also get exercise and meet people in the street. Be careful of the hot tropical sun and be sure to use sunscreen if you are out and about between 10 am and 4 pm. The best time to walk is in the early morning, the late afternoon or early evening.

# Museums and Art Galleries

The richness of Cuba's culture is reflected in its many museums, most of which are found in Havana. The city has a number of interesting museums to visit. Most of city's museums are found in beautiful colonial homes and buildings. El **Museo Numismático** displays rare coins. **El Palacio de Bellas Artes** Museum has a large collection of fine works by Cuban artists and works of art from Europe. **El Museo de la Revolución** in the presidential palace has exhibits on Cuban history and a full account of Cuba's revolution. **El Museo de Ciencias** or Museum of Science is also worth visiting. Across from the university in Vedado is the **Museo Napoleónico**. The building is more impressive than its exhibits. These are a few of the most popular museums in Havana.

There are other museums in other large towns and cities. Be sure and visit the **Ernest Hemingway Museum** seven miles southeast of Havana in the suburb of San Francisco de Paula.

The house is just the way it was when Hemingway lived there. It is full of original furnishings and possessions. Here is a partial list of the many museums in the Havana area:

| | |
|---|---|
| National Museum of Natural History | Tel: (32) 9000 |
| National Music Museum | Tel: (80) 6810 |
| Colonial Art Museum in Havana Vieja | Tel: (62) 6440 |
| Museum of Fine Arts in Havana Vieja | Tel: (62) 9042 |
| Morro-Cabana Historical Military Park | Tel: (62) 0607 |
| José Marti's Birthplace in Havana Vieja | Tel: (61) 3778 |
| Museo de la Educación | Tel: (61) 5468 |
| Decorative Arts Museum in Vedado | Tel: (32) 0924 |
| Museum of Sciences in Havana Vieja | Tel: (63) 4824 |
| Anthropological Museum at the University | Tel: (79) 3488 |
| Numismatic Museum | Tel: (61) 5857 |
| Postal Museum | Tel: (70) 5581 |
| City Museum of Havana | Tel: (61) 2876 |

Havana also has its share of art galleries. There are **Galería La Acacia** Tel: (63) 9364, **Galería del Arte Latinoamericano** Tel: (32) 5365, **Casa de las Américas** (55) 2706, **Galería Victor Manuel** (61) 2955 and **Galería Haydee Santamaría** Tel: (32) 4652 to name a few. **The newspaper Cartelera** and **Guía Cultural de la Habana** have information about exhibitions and galleries.

## Urban Parks

**The National Aquarium** is in the Miramar district of the city. There are also two zoos in Havana: The run-down **Parque Zoológico de la Havana** Tel: (81) 8915 and the **Parque Zoológico Nacional**. Tel: (44) 7613.

Havana and most cities and small towns are dotted with parks. **Parque Lenin** is Havana's largest park and recreational area. It is a huge 1600 acre park of rolling hills and popular playground with the locals about 7 miles southeast of the city. It is located next to a large lake. There is an art gallery, a riding school, an amphitheater, an open-air movie theater, a freshwater aquarium, a botanical garden, a small amusement park, cafeterias, refreshment stands and more within the boundaries of the park. On weekends it is packed with Cuban families. There are also smaller parks scattered around the metropolitan area where you can go to relax.

## Movies, Theater and Dance

By some estimates there are over 100 movie theaters in Havana. Don't expect to find movie theaters with multiple screens under one roof as in the U.S., Mexico or Costa Rica. However, it is only a matter of time before these mammoth theaters will be built, enabling you to see first-run movies. Nevertheless, many English movies are now shown at tourist resorts and hotels on special cable channels. There are a couple of good movie theatres in Havana. Admission is cheap, but the selection is limited. Currently most movies shown are from Argentina, Russia, Europe, Mexico and the U.S. Most Hollywood movies are shown a about a year after they have been released abroad. A lot of American films are pirated off satellites.

The best movie theaters are the **Cine Yara** Tel: 32-9430 in Vedado Tel:32-9430, opposite the Havana Libre Hotel, **Charles Chaplin** in Vedado Tel: 31-1101, **Cine Payret** Tel: 63-3163 opposite the Capitolio, **Cine La Rampa** in Vedado Tel:78-6146 and **Cine Acapulco** in Vedado tel; 3-9573. Listings of movies can usually be found in newspapers and on posters.

Every year Havana is the site of the **New Latin American Film Festival**. It is the most important film festival in the Spanish-speaking world. Celebrities, big shot motion picture executives and movie lovers from all over the world attend.

Since early times, live theater has always played a role in Cuban life. There are over fifty theaters in the country and several theater companies. Some of these companies perform outdoors. Havana's **Teatro Mella** (Tel:38-6961) and **Gran Teatro de la Habana** in Central Havana (Tel: 61-3078) are two of the best. There are also **Sala del Conjunto Folclórico Nacional** (Tel: 31-3467), **Teatro Bertold Brecht** (Tel: 32-9359), **Teatro Hubert de Blank** (Tel: 30-1011) and **Teatro Nacional de Cuba** (Tel:79-6011) all found in the Vedado district of Havana.

Dancing is an integral part of Cuban culture as was discussed in the section on Cuba's people. Many dance forms have originated in Cuba and every celebration includes some form of dance. The **National Ballet of Cuba** is considered one of the finest in the world. They perform occasionally at Havana's **Gran Teatro**. Each November there is an international ballet festival held in Havana. Modern dance companies and the **National Folklore Group** also perform.

Cuba has many excellent artists. There is an abundance of art galleries found in Havana. There are usually more than 20 exhibits at any one time around the city. To find listings you should look in the newspapers.

## Television and Radio

There is a special T.V. channel called the Sun channel or **Canal del Sol** which has limited English programming. A number of hotels offer satellite television from the U.S. for their guests. They show programs such as CNN, HBO, ESPN, Cinemax and MTV. With a satellite dish you can pick programs from all over the world. Very soon, RCA's Direct T.V. or another satellite company will be offering service to Cuba just as in the rest of Latin America. In case you don't know, these satellite systems are very good because they use a dish about 30 inches wide and pick up about 150 channels. We have an American friend who lives on his yacht at the Hemingway Marina. He has a satellite system and claims he can get almost every available station.

Actually, many people can pick up television stations from Miami—weather permitting—with an ordinary antenna if they live near Havana. **Cuba Visión** and **Tele Rebelde** are the country's official Spanish television networks. These stations show old American and European films, science and culture, soaps and cartoons. Since sports are very popular, a lot of games are broadcast. If you speak Spanish you can view the programs they offer.

Cuba has a couple of national radio stations. **Radio Taino** is the main station which broadcasts throughout the country in Spanish and English 24-hours a day on AM frequency. **Radio Reloj** is a 24-hour news station. English language radio stations can also be heard from the southern United States, Mexico, The Dominican Republic, Puerto Rico and Venezuela.

## Newspapers and Books

The main national daily Spanish newspaper is the *Granma*. It is the official newspaper of Cuba, is printed in five languages and can be accessed at: http://granma.cu. For tourist-oriented information in Spanish-English read the Cartelera magazine which covers many local activities. In most hotels catering to tourists, you can buy *USA Today*, *New York Times*, *The International Herlald Tribune*, *Newsweek* and *Miami Herald*. The hotel Havana Libre stocks most of these publications. There is also a selection of magazines and other reading materials in English.

Cable news network or CNN was recently given a special license to open a news bureau in Havana. Ted Turner gave Cuba the right to show CNN on Cuban television, so it was only logical CNN would be the first news bureau to be approved. Nine other news groups were also granted licenses: ABC News, CBS news, *The Miami Herald*, *The Associated Press*, *Dow Jones & Company*, *The Chicago Tribune*, *The Fort Lauderdale Sun Sentinel*, *Univision* and possibly *The New York Times*.

Despite being a country of avid readers, only a few bookstores stock titles in English. Once the country opens up to the global economy, the number of bookstores stocking books in English will increase. Someday there may even be branches of large international bookstore chains like Barnes & Noble or Borders in Havana.

The **International Bookstore** on Calle Obispo No 526 and **Librería Bella Havana** in Havana have a small selection of English books. **Moderna Poesía** (La Habana Vieja, Obispo 526 at Bernaza Tel: 62-2189) is another good bookstore. There are also a couple of hard currency shops that sell books.

Other bookstores are: **Ateneo** in Vedado between 12th and 14th Tel:36-9009; **El Siglo de Las Luces** in Centro Habana, Neptuno 521 at Aguila; **Fernando Ortiz** in Vedado,Calle L and 27th Tel:32-9653; **Luis Rogelio Nogueras** in Centro Habana, Galiuano 467 Tel: 63-8110; 1 **Palacio del Segundo Cabo** in La Habana Vieja,O'Reilly 4, at Tacón Tel: 62-8091, **Librería Cervantes** which specializes in used books, **Librería Casa de las Américas** and **Librería Centenario**. There are even occasional bookfairs where a few second-hand books in English may be found.

Havana also has many public libraries. **La Biblioteca Nacional José Martí** (at Plaza de la Revolución in Vedado Tel: 79-6091) is Havana's main public library. Other libraries are: **Biblioteca Pública Provincial Rubén Villena, Biblioteca Nacional de Ciencia y Tecnología** (The National Science and Technology Library, located in the former Capitol Building, Tel:60-3411), **Biblioteca del Instituto de Literatura y Liguística** (Institute of Literature and Linguistics Library) Tel: 74-504), **Biblioteca Memorial Juan Marinello** (Juan Marinello Memorial Library, in Nuevo Vedado Tel:34-912) and the **Biblioteca José Antonio Echevarría** (Vedado Tel:32-358) featuring books by Latin American authors. However, at present you are really better off shopping for reading materials in English abroad or trading books with other English-speaking expatriates. If you are fluent in Spanish you have nothing to worry about since there are many materials available.

There is annual Havana Book Fair held in February which is a book lovers' paradise.

While on the subject of books the name of José Martí inevitably comes up. He was Cuba's most famous writer and revolutionary leader in the country's Second War of Independence during the 1800's. Martí wrote many poems, essays and plays. He died in a battle fighting for his beliefs.

## Music, Dance and Carnival

As you know, Cuba is the cradle of tropical music. Music is the most salient feature of Cuba's culture. Cuban music is a mixture of African percussion and Spanish guitar. Dancing is an important part of Cuban music. So, if you love to dance and enjoy Latin music, Cuba is the perfect place for you to live.

*Salsa* is the best known and most popular type of Cuban music. *Mambo* and *cha-cha-cha* are older forms of Cuban music that have become popular throughout the world. No discussion of Cuban music would be complete without mentioning the most famous song to come out of Cuba—*Guantanamera*. Many international singers have popularized this song. Son is the local equivalent of country music. Celia Cruz, Xavier Cugart, Pérez Prado and Desi Arnaz are just a few of the excellent singers and musicians Cuba has produced over the years.

Recently, jazz has become very popular. Cuba has produced a string of fine international jazz musicians. They are admired all over the world for their virtuosity and creativity. Sadly, most of Cuba's better jazz musicians have left the country. You don't have to go far to hear live music. Musicians play every type of music all over the country, from clubs to concerts and even on street corners—music pervades the air.

# "Hot Havana Nights"

## By Christopher Baker

"Dark-eyed Stellas light their fellas' panatellas," said Irving Berlin, the late American composer. And how!

I had just watched, mesmerized, as pink and mauve searchlights swept over hordes of voluptuous showgirls at Havana's Tropicana night club. After the show a stunning mulatta sat down beside me. I liked her boldness, so characteristic of Cuban women. We arranged a date at La Bodeguita del Medio, Ernest Hemingway's favorite watering hole, half-a-block from the antique cathedral.

We sipped mojitos, the rum mint julep that Hemingway brought out of obscurity. They were strong, and staring into Stella's dark eyes I felt the glow of which Berlin had written.

She invited me to a soiree hosted by an intoxicated warm-hearted woman named Dulce María. Climbing a rickety staircase to the top of a dilapidated four-story building, I emerged on a rooftop overlooking the Plaza de la Catedral. Hands were extended; I was hugged warmly by Cubans I did not know. Dulce's band - Son de Cuba - was gearing up with a rumba. The rhythms pulsed across the rooftops of Old Havana. Rum and beer were passed around, and soon we were clapping and laughing beneath the star-filled sky while Dulce belted out traditional Cuban compositions, her hips swaying undulantly to the narcotic rhythms. The infectious beat lured us to dance.

It was hard to believe that the U.S. government's Trading With the Enemy Act is directed at these people. Dulce and her friends never stopped smiling.

"I want to see the stars; they're so beautiful," said my Tropicana nightingale, leading me by the hand toward the Malecón sea-front boulevard and the final seduction. It was well beyond midnight. Couples were necking openly along the Malecón. The air was languid and as we strolled we were seized by desire. My paramours white skirt glowed luminously in the moonlight and our furtive passion must have been great theater for onlookers.

Suddenly the beam of a floodlight from the castle swept over us, freezing us in flagrant delict. I recalled author Pico Iyer's line that "the tourists exciting adventures have stakes he cannot fathom." I laughed, nervously. She asked why. "This is a ridiculous situation," I said. "But everything in Cuba is ridiculous," she replied.

There are dozens of clubs which feature dancers and musicians playing salsa and congo rhythms. Cabarets are found at the **Capri Hotel** in Vedado, the **Caribe** in the Hotel Havana Libre and the **Cabaret Parisien** at the Hotel Nacional in Vedado.

There are discos at hotels and dance halls where you can dance the night away if you so desire. **Discoteca Habana Club** (Hotel Comdoro), **Habana Café** (Hotel Meliá Cohiba), the **Ache** at Cuba's new **Hotel Meliá Cohiba** and the **Palacio de Salsa** are the "in" places to dance and are also fun. **Arcos de Cristal** next to the **Tropicana** is another good bet. You can also dance at **Club Turquino** at the Havana Libre Hotel; the **Discoteca del Hotel Copacabana** in the Miramar district; **Discoteca Habana Club** in the Hotel Comodore in Miramar; **El Elegante Bar** at the hotel Rivera in Vedado; **La Tasca Española** at the Marina Hemingway; **Piano Bar Neptuno** at the Hotel Neptuno in Miramar; and **Skiper** video-bar at the Hotel Capri in Vedado district.

Good news! A Mexican company in a joint venture was recently given the rights to establish a **Hard Rock Cafe** franchise in Havana. It is only a matter of time before other trendy international chains come to Cuba.

You can hear Latin music performed at **La Casa de Tova** in Havana. Jazz enthusiasts can hear live jazz at the Jazz Café in Vedado, **Café Turqino** in the Habana Libre Hotel Hotel Riviera and **1830 Club**. The annual Havana International Jazz Festival is held in mid-February.

Before the Cuban Revolution, Havana was the Las Vegas of the Caribbean because of its great entertainment, night clubs and musical reviews—some shows still exist. The most famous night club act is still found at the world famous outdoor **Tropicana Night Club** Tel: (537) 0110. Performances are held in the open air. The reviews and costumes rival Las Vegas and the atmosphere is unsurpassed. All big hotels have their own cabarets and night clubs. **Cabaret Copa Room** (Hotel Habana Riviera), **Cabaret**

**Parsien** (Hotel Nacional), the **Cabaret Nacional** also offer excitement.

Most hotels and restaurants offer a variety of exotic beverages. **The Turquino Bar** at the Hotel Havana Libre has panoramic views of the city. The **Bodeguita del Medio** and the **Floridita** were two favorite watering holes of Hemingway. **La Taberna del Galeon** on the Plaza de Armas is a good tourist bar. Along the scenic Malecón you can drink at the **1830** bar or a couple of smaller establishments.

Carnival in Cuba is an old tradition dating back several hundred years. This usually takes place after the sugar harvest or *zafra*. The best carnivals take place in Cuba's two main cities of Havana and Santiago de Cuba. Havana's carnival is held in mid-February and lasts an entire week. The whole Malecón area fills up with Cubans and foreigners. *Comparsas*— a type of street dancing or performance from a neighborhood—are part of carnival and can be seen at different times and locations during the year.

## $hopping

For the time being, shopaholics will be disappointed if they expect to find shopping areas like Beverly Hill's Rodeo drive or large U.S. or Canadian style malls in Cuba. Havana does have its share of open-air markets, cigar stores, souvenir shops, art galleries and upscale jewelry stores. Cimex operates stores all over Havana which sell all kinds of Western products. Galerías de Paseo in Vedado also has imported goods.

The seeds of American suburbia have begun to take root. The **Plaza Carlos III Mall**, four stories of shops and fast-food outlets around a central atrium, opened up in the center of Havana, within blocks of the Plaza of the Revolution. Galerías de Paseo, across the street from the Hotel Meliá Cohiba, is an upscale shopping center catering to wealthy Cubans and Americans.

Benneton, the trendy clothing company, already has representation and retail stores in Havana. It is only a matter of time before other lines of brand clothing are available in Cuba.

As the country enters the world market things are bound to change. More and more foreign goods are available in Cuba today. However, for now you are better off picking up what you need while in the States, Canada, Europe or a neighboring country like the Dominican Republic.

As you know, one of the advantages of living in Cuba is its proximity to the United States. Eventually shopping will be almost as convenient as living on the Mexican or Canadian borders where foreigners cross frequently to shop. On a short shopping trip to Miami you will be able to buy essentials as sundries, medicines, clothing and other products you can't live without or which can't be purchased in Cuba.

While shopping in the states or a neighboring country it will be a good idea to stock up on cotton clothing. The more cotton clothing you have the more comfortable you will be. In tropical areas cotton is the coolest type of clothing you can wear. We also recommend hats if you intend to walk under the hot tropical sun. Don't forget to have several pairs of cool walking shoes. You might think about waterproofing them for the rainy season. Don't forget a good umbrella, since tropical rain is warm and raincoats will keep you dry but make you sweat like crazy.

## Spectator Sports and Games

Cubans are avid sports fans and interested in a variety of spectator sports. Cuba is viewed by many as "the best little sports machine in the world" because of the number of outstanding athletes it has produced over the years, including three-time Olympic boxing champion Teofilo Stevenson and Javier Sotomayor, the world record holder in the high jump and only man to clear 8 feet in the event. Most young people are encouraged to participate in some kind of athletic endeavor.

Since it was introduced in the early 1900's, baseball has been the favorite sport of Cuba. Many Cubans have distinguished themselves as professional players in the big leagues. Cuba's amateur teams are some of the best in the world. Almost every city and town has a stadium where baseball games take place. Cuba's major league is called **La Liga Nacional**. Over the last few years there has been a string of defections of Cuba's most notable baseball players including Orlando "El Duque" Hernández, his brother Livan and Rolando Arrojo to name a few.

The main baseball season runs from December to June. Havana's main baseball stadium is the 60,000 seat Estadio Latinoamericano located in Vedado. Havana has two national teams, Industriales and Metropolitanos. Everyone should attend a lively baseball game in Cuba to savor the wonderful atmosphere.

Havana also has adequate sports facilities and even hosted the Pan-American Games. Boxing is also popular. A long line of amateur champions have come out of Cuba. Soccer enjoys some following but has not caught on as in other Latin American countries. Basketball is the most popular court game among Cuba's black community. Almost all high schools and colleges have teams. Cuban volleyball teams are outstanding. Cycling has become popular and there are several cycling clubs in the Havana area.

Most hotels have swimming pools which are open to non guests. There are a couple of public pools at Parque Lenin. **The Club Habana** Tel: (24) 5700 and the **Marina** have excellent pool facilities which are open to nonmembers for a small fee.

Surprisingly, there are two bowling alleys: one at the **Havana Golf Club** Tel: (55) 8746 and another at the **Hotel Kohly** in Vedado Tel: (24) 0240.

As we mentioned, there are two golf courses in the country; one in Havana and another at the Varadero resort. More courses are bound to be built in the future. Public tennis facilities are limited but most resort areas have courts .

Although not spectator sports, chess and especially dominoes are widely played and enjoyed be Cubans. Dominoes is second only to baseball in popularity. Some Cubans insist that it is even more popular. It was originally brought from the Andalusian part of Spain.

## Gambling

Gambling is a deep rooted Cuban tradition. Before 1959 you could bet on cockfighting, jai alai, horse racing or frequent casinos run by the American mafia and gangsters like Myer Lansky. Presently, there is no form of legalized gambling or betting as existed in the pre-Castro days. There is, however, a form of underground lottery. Cuba's illegal lottery is called la *bolita*. Everyday Cubans place their bets clandestinely with a *listero* or type of bookie. Since there is no longer an official Cuban lottery, winning numbers come from abroad. The last two digits of the five-digit Venezuelan lottery become the wining numbers in Cuba. We have also heard rumors that there is a another form of illegal gambling at a private club near the Hemingway Marina. However, at present we can't substantiate the information.

## Finding Companionship

If you are single and seeking companionship, Cuba just may be the place for you. Cuban women have a reputation for being well-educated and beautiful. They are famous for their shapely *derriéres* . Most Cuban women are industrious and have taken an active role in the workplace in recent years.

Like other Latin American women they tend to be more warm-hearted and eternally devoted than their North American counterparts. The women like foreign men, since Cuban men are usually too macho in their ways and unfaithful to their girl friends and wives.

Unfortunately, hard times have given birth to a revival of prostitution and a class of unscrupulous female gold diggers or jinteras that prey on foreign men. Many can be found hanging out in hotel lobbies like the Riviera and discotheques, on the prowl for foreigners.

This is not to say you can't find sincere women and matrimony in Cuba. However, there are some precautions you should take to ensure a women is really interested in you and not your wallet. You will save yourself a lot of grief and heartache in the long run. Beware of women you meet in bars, in discotheques, in the street or who seem overly assertive, forward and eager to get involved. Any women who is constantly trying to get you to buy her things or asking for money is not worthwhile. You will be smart to give any relationship time to develop and not be impulsive.

The key is finding a nice, traditional Latin women and avoiding getting involved with "bad girls." Cuba has plenty of working girls and hustlers. They hang out at popular tourist areas, bars and discos specifically to pick up guys. They also ride buses and go to stores. So, just because you have met a nice girl in a typical working girl hangout, doesn't mean you have met a quality person. If you know what to look for, they are easy to spot.

Many men have knowingly and unknowingly married bad women. Working girls are usually honest and will directly ask you for money. The hustlers are more dangerous because their agenda is to really "take you to the cleaners" and they do not rule out marrying you to achieve their objective. Some men have lost everything from airline tickets that are cashed instead of used, to large sums of money the girls claim they need for a variety of reason, and more. These are the women who contribute to the bad stories you may hear about Latin women. So falling in love with a bad girl will typically lead to a lot of heart ache and problems. Unfortunately they are the easiest girls to meet in Latin America and many men fall into this trap.

Be assured that a very small number of these women will become good wives, find religion, etc. So in all fairness, one shouldn't condemn them, but rather caution men as to the problems they may encounter with these types of women. They are often women who have been sexually abused at a very young age so the problem is deeply rooted. So, your realistic chances of converting them are very slim; no matter how gorgeous the girl is, it is just not worth it.

The best way to spot a bad girl is by her profile. They seldom have a job, never live with their parents, never have phone numbers and never invite you to their home or introduce you to their friends or family. They do not want to leave any trail for you to track them down later. They typically come from very poor backgrounds and have very little education.

They are quite aggressive and like to target older men. Often they speak a little English and will start up a conversation with you or smile at you until you make the first move. They will appear to be friendly and sincerely interested in you. They are always attractive or very young. They will always ask you for your phone number. The best way to politely get rid of these women is to ask them to loan you a little money. You will immediately see their interest disappear.

A big misconception about Latin females is that they prefer older men. This seems to be the case in only about 30% of the women. Most Latin women meet a boy in high school and are only interested in guys their own age. However, about 30% do seriously prefer older men. I have met many people who are successfully married to women 10 to 25 years younger than them.

Nice Latin women from traditional family backgrounds are raised to take care of their men. They can be quite possessive and jealous at times. But this is only because they are very emotional and deeply in love with their men. They tend to seek out long term relationships, starting at a very young age.

When approached by strangers, they are friendly and helpful by nature; this is their culture. All Latinos value making new friends. Americans and other foreigners often mistake this friendliness and think the woman has romantic interest in them. But actually, respectable women have no serious interest in dating a tourist, who they perceive as being in the country for a short time and primarily interested in sex.

In order for the woman to develop any romantic interest in you at all, they have to first know from a trusted third party that you are looking for a long term relationship. After a brief encounter, a decent woman will never ask for your phone number. If you ask for her phone number, she will always give you the wrong number in order to avoid appearing rude. Nice girls live with their parents and would never want to have strange guys calling their houses. From a romantic interest point of view, quality Latin women are difficult to meet. They have no interest in casually dating many different guys.

If the woman is convinced you are seriously looking for a long term relationship she will then start to show interest in getting to know you better.

Even if you do find your ideal mate, you should realize that there are many cultural differences which can lead to all sorts of problems down the road, especially if you don't speak fluent Spanish.

Currently Cuba doesn't offer internationally accepted marriages for foreign citizens marrying foreign citizens. However, marriages between Cubans and foreigners are legal. Marriage is one of the few requirements for travel from Cuba by Cuban citizens.

Many foreigners, especially Europeans, have married Cuban women. Due to the country's many economic hardships, most Cuban women will jump at the chance to marry a foreigner in order to improve their lifestyle. Unfortunately marrying a Cuban woman and getting her out of the country is rather difficult at present. This process is virtually impossible for U.S. citizens due to the embargo.

Basically the process goes like this. First you have to your country's embassy or consulate in Cuba. Likewise you need to go Cuba immigration to see what paperwork is involved there. This whole process will cost around $1500 and can take four months or longer to get everything in order.

Currently American citizens cannot not bring their spouse directly back to the U.S. since most Americans are prohibited from travelling there at the present time. However, there is a way to get around this snag. If an American is a resident of a third country like Mexico or Costa Rica, you can take your spouse to that third country and then apply for a visa to the states.

However, you should go to your country's embassy or consulate in Cuba. Likewise you need to go to Cuba's Immigration Department to see what paperwork is involved. This whole process will cost around $1500 and may take four months or longer to get everything in order.

Currently it is difficult for American citizens to bring their spouses directly back to the U.S. since most Americans are prohibited from travelling to Cuba. However, there is a way to get around this snag. If an American is a resident of a third country like Mexico or Costa Rica, you can take your spouse to that third country and then apply for a visa to the States.

We recently interviewed an American citizen from San Diego who claims that the best method to get your future spouse out of Cuba and to the States is by obtaining a Fiancé Visa which usually takes three to four months. You have to go to the U.S. Interests Section to apply. He sweares this is the fast track method since it sometimes takes 12 to 14 months to get a marriage visa.

Another method is to marry in Cuba and get your future spouse a visa to a third country. Once there, you can marry your fiancé and get her a visa to U.S. if you are a legal resident of the third country. All of these stringent regulations should be relaxed for Americans once relations are normalized between the U.S. and Cuba. An organization at www.gocuba/marriages can help organize your marriage and assist you with all of the bureaucratic steps you need to take.

If you want a pictorial introduction to Cuba's beautiful women buy a copy of Christopher Baker's the soon-to-be-released, *Women of the Caribbean*. This beautifully illustrated book portrays the glamour of the most stunning women of Cuba as well as women from other countries of the Caribbean.

Mr. Baker is the award-winning author of the best-selling *Cuba Handbook* and the recently-released *Havana Handbook*.

# CHAPTER 5

## SHORT CUTS FOR LEARNING SPANISH

If you plan to live in Cuba it is in your best interest to learn Spanish—the more the better. Frankly, you will be at a disadvantage, somewhat handicapped, and probably always considered a foreigner to some degree without Spanish.

Part of the fun of living in another country is being able to communicate with the locals. Spanish will help you do your banking, find your way around and may even assist you in your romantic endeavors. You will save time and money when shopping and looking for bargains. Spanish will keep people from taking advantage of you and make it easier to deal with the kind of stifling bureaucracy found in Latin America. If you plan to work or do business, Spanish is indispensable. Learning Spanish will lead to a much more rewarding lifestyle and open the door for new and rewarding experiences.

Spanish is also essential if you wind up getting romantically involved with a Cuban. Under these circumstances you will need a basic knowledge of Spanish to facilitate communication. Let's face it, even if two people speak the same language, at times it can be difficult to have a successful relationship. Over the years while residing in Costa Rica the author has watched many relationships fail between Spanish and English speakers due to poor communication.

The best thing a person can do is to begin studying Spanish before moving to Cuba to get a head start. We have lost track of the number of times we have heard English speakers lament not having learned the language before moving to a Spanish speaking country.

Try enrolling at a local night school or community college. Better yet, take private lessons from a native speaker. One-on-one instruction can truly speed-up the learning process.

Once you have learned the basics and get a feel for the language you can then watch Spanish T.V. programs, listen to Spanish radio and music and read as often as possible to increase your vocabulary.

Another excellent way to learn Spanish is to take a "language vacation" to a Spanish speaking country. You should then make arrangements to live with a local family who speaks little or, preferably, no English. This way you will be forced to develop your language skills. Presently it is easier to study Spanish in counties like Guatemala, Costa Rica or Mexico. Due to logistics, the availability of established language schools and comfort you may opt to study in one of these countries instead of Cuba.

There are very good language study programs in Antigua, Guatemala. The town's number one business is teaching Spanish to students. People come from all over the world to take advantage of the low-cost classes. The language schools in the area offer tailor made courses for all levels, one-on-one intensive instruction and home-stay with local families. The best school is the **Academia Española**, 3 Avenida, #15, Antigua, Guatemala. Tel/Fax: (502-9) 320344.

The town of Cuernavaca Mexico—located near Mexico City—also has numerous language schools and programs akin to those offered in Antigua. The beautiful town of **San Miguel de Allende** in central Mexico has language classes at the **Instituto Allende**. If you are interested in studying Spanish in Mexico, call **International Summerstays** at 800-274-6007 or **Language Studies Abroad** at 800-424-5522.

Peaceful Costa Rica has about two dozen Spanish schools from which to choose. **Centro Liguistico Conversa** offers a conversational program with homestay included. For more information write to: Apdo. 17-1007, Centro Colón, San José, Costa Rica. Tel: (506) 221-76-49, Fax: (506) 233-2418.

If you decide you want to study in Cuba there are several programs which currently offer courses. **Mercadu** Tel: 33-3893 Fax: 33-3028 located in the Vedado district of Havana is a place to start. They offer intensive courses through the University of Havana for any level. **Centro de Idiomas para Estranjeros José Martí**, Avenida 3 #402, Miramar, Havana Tel/Fax: 33-1697 also has courses for foreigners. Finally **Global Exchange** in the U.S., 2017 Mission St., Suite 303, San Francisco, CA 94114, Tel: 800-497-1994 , www.globalexchange.com has language courses at the **José Martí Language Center**.

Spanish is not a difficult language to learn. With a little self-discipline and motivation, anyone can acquire a basic Spanish survival vocabulary of between 200-3000 words in a relative short period of time. Many Spanish words are similar enough to English so you can figure out their meanings by just looking at them: *tractor*-tractor, *presidente*-president, *horrible*-horrible, *natural*-natural, *tropical*-tropical, *chocolate*-chocolate, *hotel*-hotel, *sociable*-sociable etc.

The Spanish alphabet is almost like the English one, with a few minor exceptions. Pronunciation is easier than English because you say the words like they look like they should be said. Spanish grammar is somewhat complicated, but can be made easier if you are familiar with English grammar and find a good teacher.

Practicing with a native speaker is by far the best way to improve your Spanish because you can learn how the language is spoken in everyday conversations. It will also help you improve your accent. You will learn new words and expressions not ordinarily found in your standard dictionary or grammar book. If you are lucky enough to find a Cuban teacher you will really have a big advantage.

Listening to language cassettes can also improve your Spanish. There are many cassettes on the market. Each claims to use a particular method guaranteed to teach you the language. At the end of this section we list some of the cassettes that are found in your local bookstore.

The most complete cassette course is produced by the **Foreign Service Institute of the State Department** (Call 1-800-243-1234 for information). This course consists of three levels with each being the equivalent of one year of college Spanish. It is used to train government personnel and diplomats before they go overseas. These tapes will give you a solid foundation in spoken Spanish, however, it is very extensive and requires a long-term commitment and dedication to profit from the benefits this program has to offer.

Speaking of cassettes, if you are a beginner with little or no knowledge of Spanish, you should purchase the one-of-a-kind book, The *Spanish Survival Course* and accompanying 90-minute cassette advertised in this book. It is designed especially for people planning to live in Spanish speaking countries like Cuba. It makes learning basic Spanish easy because the student learns the natural way by listening and repeating like a child without grammar. By no means is it a complete Spanish course, but it will give the student a large enough dose of the language to handle most everyday situations.

# Super Tips For Learning Spanish
## By Christopher Howard M.A.

1) Build you vocabulary. Try to learn a minimum of five new words daily.

2) Watch Spanish TV programs. Keep a note pad by your side and jot down new words and expressions. Later use the dictionary to look up any words and expressions you don't understand.

(3) Pay attention to the way the locals speak the Language.

(4) Listen to Spanish music.

(5) Talk with as many different Spanish speakers as you can. You will learn something from everyone. Carry a small notebook and write down new words when you hear them.

(6) Read aloud in Spanish for five minutes a day to improve your accent.

(7) Try to imitate native speakers when you talk.

(8) Don't be afraid of making mistakes.

(9) Practice using your new vocabulary words in complete sentences.

10) When you learn something new, form a mental picture to go along with it—visualize the action.

11) Try to talk in simple sentences. Remember, your Spanish is not at the same level as your English, so simplify what you are trying to say.

12) If you get stuck or tongue-tied, try using nouns instead of complete sentences.

13) Remember Spanish and English are more similar than different. There are many cognates (words that are the same of almost the same in both languages).

14) Learn all of the basic verb tenses and memorize the important regular and irregular verbs in each tense.

15) Study Spanish grammar, but don't get bogged down in it.

16) Read the newspaper. The comic strips are great because they have a lot of dialog.

17) It takes time to learn another language. Don't be impatient. Most English speakers are in a hurry to learn foreign languages and get frustrated easily because the process is slow. Study a little bit everyday, be dedicated, persist and most of all enjoy the learning process.

¡Buena suerte! Good luck!

# Getting a Head Start
## By Christopher Howard M.A.

If you are seriously considering moving to a Latin American country, you should begin to study Spanish as soon as possible.

Here are a few suggestions that will give you a head start in learning the language. Look for some type of Spanish course that emphasizes conversation as well as grammar and enroll as soon as possible. University extension, junior colleges and night schools usually offer a wide range of Spanish classes.

You should also consider studying at a private language school like Berlitz if there is one near where you reside. Many of these schools allow the students to work at their own pace.

Another excellent way to learn Spanish, if you can afford it, is to hire a private language tutor. Like private schools this type of instruction can be expensive, but is very worthwhile. The student has the opportunity of working one-on-one with a teacher and usually progresses much faster than in a large group situation.

If you happen to reside in an area where there are no schools that offer Spanish classes, you should go to your local bookstore and purchase some type of language cassette. This way, at least you will have a chance to learn correct pronunciation and train your ear by listening to how the language is spoken.

Listening to radio programs in Spanish and watching Spanish television are other ways to learn the language, if you are fortunate enough to live in an area where there are some of these stations.

You can also spend your summer or work vacations studying Spanish in Mexico or Costa Rica. This way you will experience language in real life situations. These language vacations can be enjoyable and rewarding experiences.

Finally, try befriending as many native Spanish speakers as you can who live in the area where you reside. Besides making new friends, you will have someone to practice with and ask questions about the language.

By following the advice above and making an effort to learn the language, you should be able to acquire enough basic language skills to prepare you for living in a Spanish speaking country. Best of all, you will acquire the life-long hobby of learning a new language in the process.

Lonely Planet Publications released a book on Cuban Spanish in early 2001. It is mainly geared for the traveler and gives basic survival phrases and vocabulary.

Although a number of Cubans speak English, Russian or French, the official language is Spanish. Cuban Spanish is basically the same as standard Castilian Spanish, but there are a few minor differences you will have to get used to.

The Cuban dialect can be very difficult to understand because the people speak very fast, slurring almost mumbling some words as if they we talking with a mouth full of food. On top of that, Cubans tend not to pronounce the letter "s" in most words. For instance, instead of saying, "¿Cómo está usted?" (How are you?), they say, "¿Cómo etá?". Many linguists say that people who live at low altitudes tend to speak Spanish faster because they need less oxygen to speak than those people living at higher elevations. Perhaps this is why the Cuban people speak so quickly. As for not pronouncing the letter "s", this phenomenon seems to be part of a regional Caribbean dialect. The people of Puerto Rico and the Domincan Republic also eliminate the letter "s".

If you listen to Cubans speak Spanish you will notice they use a lot of expressions not heard in other countries of Latin America. These expressions and words are called, cubanismos. The majority of these phrases are not found in Spanish dictionaries and sometimes have double meanings.

Here is a list of some of the most common phrases:

*aguaje* — a downpour

*asere*— friend

*babujal* — an evil spirit

*bici* — bicycle

*bohío* — hut built of wood and palm leaves

*bucha* — a despicable person

*caballería* — old Spanish system for measuring land

*carjal* — a lot of money

*carranchoso* — rough

*coger botella* or *hacer botella* — hitch hiking.

*espejuelos* — glasses

*fiñe* — child

*gomas* — tires

*guagua* (wah-wah) — bus

*guajiro* —a country person

*gusano* — an unpatriotic person

*jama* — food

*jinetero/a* — gold digger or street hustler

*mangonear*— to manipulate

*máquinas*— old cars used for taxis

*menudo* — change(coins)

*mima* — mom

*paluchero* — a charlatan

*pavana* — a beating

*pepe* — a foreigner

*pipo* — dad

*la pureta* — mother

If you wish to learn Cuban phrases, we suggest you buy any of the Cuban phrase books we list below. They are packed with hundreds of words and expressions peculiar to Cuba. You can get a head start on learning Cuban Spanish by studying these books. The downside is that the first three books are written in Spanish. Unless you are an advanced Spanish student you probably won't understand the phrases and words they contain.

*Diccionario de Cubanismos* Más Usuales, by José Sánchez-Boudy is a series of volumes packed full of idioms and slang.

*Refranero Familiar*, by Concepción Teresa Alzola has many proverbs and sayings used by the Cuban people.

*Así Hablaba Cuba*, by Luis Pérez López excolumnist for Miami's El Nuevo Herald. This guide has over 3,000 Cuban expressions. To order write: P.O. Box 720354, Miami, Fl 33172 or call (305) 226- 8776 or Fax: (305) 226-8709.

Here are a few other good cassette packages you can find in most bookstores:

*Berlitz Language Cassette* . Berlitz Publications. ISBN 2-8315 0888-6.

*Living Language Fast and Easy*. Cram Publishers Inc., New York, NY. ISBN 0-517-58579-0.

*Spanish at a Glance*, by Barron's Publications. 113 Crossway Park Dr. Woodbury, NY 11797.

*Spanish on the Go*, Comes with two cassettes you can take with you anywhere—while jogging, walking etc. Barron's Publications. ISBN 0-8120-7829-2.

*Talk Spanish Today* 2470 Impala Dr., Carsbad, CA 92008. Call 800-748-54804.

Below is a list of the best books available to help you learn Spanish. Most can be purchased or ordered from any bookstore.

*Barron's Basic Spanish Grammar*, by Christopher Kendris. An in-depth study of Spanish grammar for serious students.

*Barron's Spanish Idioms* by Eugene Savaia and Lynn W. Winget. This book has more than 2,000 idiomatic words and expressions. It is a helpful handbook for students of Spanish, tourists and business people who want to increase their general comprehension of the language.

*Barron's 1001 Pitfalls in Spanish.* by Julianne Dueber. This guide points to the most common errors students make and shows how to correct them.

*Barron's Spanish Vocabulary*, also by Julianne Dueber. A good book for building vocabulary.

*Dictionary of Spoken Spanish Words, Phrases and Sentences.* Dover Publications Inc., New York, NY. ISBN 0-486-20495-2. This is the best of all phrase dictionaries. It contains over 18,000 immediately usable sentences and idioms. We recommend it highly.

*Guide to Spanish Idioms*, by Raymond H. Pierson. Passport Books, 4255 West Touchy Ave, Chicago, Illinois, 60646. Contains over 2,500 expressions to help you speak like a native.

*Just Enough Business Spanish*, Passport Books. Full of phrases to help the businessman.

*Just Enough Spanish.* . Passport books. ISBN 0-8442-9500-0. As the title implies, this phrase book shows how to get by in most situations.

*Madrigal's Magic Key to Spanish* Dell Publishing Group , 666 Fifth Ave, New York, NY 10103. Provides an easy method of learning Spanish based on the many similarities between Spanish and English. This book is a "must" for the beginner.

*Nice n' Easy Spanish Grammar*, by Sandra Truscott. Passport Books. Basic grammar.

*Talking Business in Spanish*, by Bruce Fryer and Hugo J. Faria. Barron's Educational Series. Has over 3,000 business terms and phrases. A must for any person planning to do business in the Spanish speaking world.

*A New Reference Grammar of Modern Spanish*, by John Butt and Carmen Benjamin. NTC Publishing Group. This one of the best reference books ever written in Spanish grammar. It is very easy to use and understand.

*Breaking Out of Beginning Spanish*, by Joseph J. Keenan. University of Texas Press. This helpful book is written by a native English speaker who learned Spanish the hard way. It contains hundreds of practical tips.

*Cassell's Colloquial Spanish*, by A. Byron Gerrard. Macmillam. This book is full of useful information.

*Hot Spanish for Guys and Gals*, BabelCom, Inc., New York, NY. Spanish phrases that will help both sexes with their love life.

*Spanish for Gringos*, by WilliamC. Harvey. Barron's Press. This book will help you improve your Spanish.

*Household Spanish*, by William C. Harvey. Barron's Press. A user-friendly book especially for English-speakers who need to communicate with Spanish-speaking employees.

*Latin-American Spanish Dictionary,* by David Gold. Ballantine Books. A good dictionary of Spanish used in Latin America.

*The New World English/Spanish Dictionary,* by Salvatore Ramondino. A Signet Book. Another excellent dictionary of Latin American Spanish.

*Webster's New World Spanish Dictionary,* by Mike Gonzalez. Prentice Hall. Also covers Latin American usage.

# CHAPTER 6

## LIVING IN CUBA

## What to Expect

Before moving to Cuba, it is advisable to spend time there on a trial basis to see if it is the place for you. You should stay a couple months or longer so you can experience Cuban life as it is. Remember, visiting Cuba as a tourist is quite different from living there. The success rate of adjustment among Americans and other foreigners is not nearly as high as might be expected, so it is a good idea to "test the waters" before moving to Cuba or any foreign country permanently.

It is good to visit for extended periods during both the wet and dry seasons. This way you will have an idea of what the country is like at all times of the year. During your visits, talk to as many foreign residents as you can and gather as much information as possible before making your final decision.

The last step in making your decision is to try living there for at least a year. That is sufficient time to get an idea of what living in Cuba is really like and what problems may confront you while trying to adapt to living in a new culture. Some people may have to spend a couple of years in Cuba to discover whether they can live in a culture with different customs. Either way, a prolonged stay may also help you adjust to the climate and new foods.

You may decide you are more suited for seasonal living or, as they say, 'wintering ' in Cuba for a few months a year. A number of people spend the summer in Canada or the U.S. and the winter in the tropics—where it is actually summer—so they can enjoy the best of both worlds or the endless summer. By living in two places, they won't have to sever ties with their home country.

Whether you will choose to reside in Cuba full- or part-time, keep in mind the cultural differences and new customs you will encounter. Life in Cuba will be very different to what you are probably used to. If you expect all things to be the same as they are in the U.S., you are deceiving yourself. The concepts of time and punctuality are not important in Latin America. It is not unusual and not considered in bad taste for a person to arrive late for a business appointment or dinner engagement. This custom can be incomprehensible and infuriating to North Americans but will not change since it is a deep-rooted tradition.

There are numerous other examples of cultural differences you should be aware of if you are seriously considering living in Cuba. Driving habits and traffic rules are not always the same as in other countries. Tipping and even bribery are expected to ensure good service and to guarantee things will get done. Bureaucracy tends to move at a snail's pace, which can also be maddening to foreigners. Since most Americans are always in a hurry they tend to feel frustrated by the dilatory nature of many things in Latin America. In addition, the Latin mentality, machismo, Latin logic, traditions, different laws and ways of doing business, seem incomprehensible at times. You will notice countless examples of cultural idiosyncrasies after you have spent some time in Cuba.

Cultural shock is the term used to describe the reaction most people experience when they move for a long period of time to a new culture which is very different from their own. Being cut off from familiar things causes the phenomenon. Anyone entering a new environment will experience cultural shock to some degree. No matter how psychologically secure you are, some cultural shock in your new situation will confront you. Small discomforts and adversities can easily grow in importance. Many people experience homesickness, boredom, frustration and even illness. How you will like Cuba really depends on your attitude and your willingness to adapt to living in a foreign country.

Americans and Canadians are apt to view their way of doing things as better than they are done in other parts of the world. Since every culture is different, there is no "right way" of doing things. The more "cultural baggage" and preconceptions you leave behind the easier it will be for you to adjust. The best thing you can do is respect the different cultural values, be understanding, have patience and go with the flow. Also, do your homework before moving to the country, know your new country and follow all of the advice we offer in this book. Learning Spanish will ease your way.

Whatever you do don't play the role of the "Ugly American" by displaying embarrassing behavior and trying to impose your way of doing thing on the locals. Don't stereotype them and refrain from making disparaging remarks.

Making a change in your life can be refreshing, rewarding and stimulating. However, most people tend to resist change. Our advice is to try experiencing all that Cuba has to offer.

You will meet new people while residing in a foreign country. For some strange reason expatriates seem to gravitate towards each other. People who you would not normally associate with at home become instant friends when living abroad. So, making friends shouldn't be a problem. Try developing a whole network of friends for support. Being around other foreigners with a common cultural bond will make your new home seem less foreign.

For those of you who are lucky enough to be living with your family, nostalgia will be less of a factor. If you are the type of person who doesn't make the effort to meet people, who waits for things to happen, you will probably find it disappointing to live abroad. You will have to take a positive approach to create a constructive lifestyle for yourself in Cuba.

If you are retired or just taking a hiatus and have a lot of spare time on your hands, you must make an effort to stay active. In Chapter 4 there are activities to keep you busy. If you feel bored or at lose ends now, you might feel more so when living abroad. So, use your idle time wisely by getting involved. Spanish is a good way to spend your spare time. This is a lifetime project, will keep you occupied and open the door to many exciting new adventures.

Above all, Spanish will help you understand your new culture and make living abroad easier. For an adult starting from scratch, learning a new language is difficult, but can be done if you make an effort. You will certainly have enough time. Just a few minutes a day makes a difference. If you never learn Spanish you will probably be able to get by since many Cubans living in cities speak English. However, you will be missing out on a lot. Words, phrases, sentences and songs pave the way for many new and rewarding experiences. You will be surprised how much you can learn about your host country and improve your lifestyle in the process.

Be aware that you may miss many of the conveniences and activities of home—hobbies, friends, luxuries, lack of mobility, stores, your favorite T.V. programs and other familiar items. What you have to do is substitute new activities and find new hobbies. If you stay active you will adjust easily. For example, if you are an avid reader you can form a book club. Those people who like to walk can organize a walking or hiking club.

Get out and explore your neighborhood and city. You will discover restaurants, theaters, stores and other places where people gather. Try all forms of public transportation to become more mobile and discover new areas. Studying the history, politics, poetry, music and dance will help keep you busy and enable you to better understand your new culture. Remember living abroad is a trade-off: you won't have everything you had from where you came.

Food may pose a major adjustment. So, again, learn to substitute. It is also exciting to discover new foods and dishes. As we state in the next section, Cuba has many exotic dishes and native foods from which to choose. Since the U.S. is so close, you will eventually be able to pick up non-perishable items on shopping trips abroad.

Under the stress of living in a strange land some people turn to drinking as a coping mechanism. Don't fall into this trap.

You should also be aware that it is our comparative wealth that separates us from people in the third world. No matter what your present station in life, most Cubans will view you as a millionaire.

Don't count on finding work in Cuba. It is difficult for the locals to make ends meet let alone for a foreigner finding work. There are investments for those people lucky enough to have sufficient capital to invest. But people thinking they can find work to support themselves are dreaming. It is best to have an external income like a pension, annuity or savings interests. This is not meant to discourage you, but to paint a realistic picture of the work situation.

Living in a foreign country is exciting but poses many obstacles for newcomers. Don't expect everything to go smoothly at first or be perfect. By taking the advice throughout this book and adjusting to the many new challenges, you will be able to enjoy all of Cuba's wonders and have a successful lifestyle.

# food And Drink

Part of the excitement of living abroad is discovering new foods and beverages. In Cuba you will find your eating habits will probably change once you have had the opportunity to savor the native cuisine. Cuba, like every country in the world, has its own style of cooking or comida típica. Cuban dishes are a mixture of Spanish and African cooking combined with fruits and vegetables native to the island.

One of the most popular dishes is *moros y cristianos* (literally 'Moors and Christians') consisting of rice and black beans. *Picadillo* is a dish made of ground beef and assorted vegetables. *Congrí* (rice and kidney beans) and *frijoles dormidos* (sleeping beans) are other popular bean dishes. *Arroz con pollo*, chicken and rice, is also widely consumed. *Ajiaco*, a type of rice vegetable stew and a little of everything else is very tasty. *Pollo asado* (roast chicken) and *cerdo asado* (roast pork) are also popular dishes. *Empanadas* which are pies filled with meat and very good.

Because Cuba is surrounded by the sea, there is a variety of seafood from which to choose. One of the most delicious dishes is *sopa marinera*. It is a mixture of different seafoods in a soup base. Lobster, shrimp, and other varieties such as grouper and red snapper abound. Chinese and Italian food are also part of the Cuban diet.

Cuba has a large selection of tropical fruits and vegetables which are most often combined and eaten with other foods. *Yucas* (cassava root), *ñames* (yams) and *chayotes* are some of the most common vegetables. *Palmito*, palm heart, is often found in salads.

The most widely consumed fruits are: pineapple, *papaya*, *guayaba*, and *bananas*. The latter are used to make *plátanos maduros* (fried sweet bananas) and *tostones* (fried green banana chips). *Fufú* is boiled green bananas mashed into a paste and seasoned with salt.

Since Cuba produces sugar, it is not surprising that Cubans have developed a sweet tooth for a number of sugar based desserts. Most Cuban desserts are very sweet. *Churros* (a type of straight doughnut), are a favorite, *flan* (a type of Spanish custard), *dulce de leche, buñuelos* and *coco quemado* are typical Cuban desserts. *Granizado* is a dessert made of shaved ice with sugary syrup much like a snow cone. The renowned **Coppelia** ice cream parlor serves the best ice cream in Cuba.

If you have a craving for your favorite food from the States, there are food stores which already sell U.S. food products for dollars. Some of the better known brands available are: Campells Soup, Heinz, Del Monte, Libby's, Kraft, Bumble Bee, Progreso, Uncle Ben's, Planters, Gerber, Motts and Purina to name a few.

Coffee and rum are the two most popular beverages. It is impossible to talk about Cuban cuisine without mentioning Cuba's excellent coffee. It is usually served very strong and following meals or by itself. *Café cubano* is a type of coffee that is brewed differently and served like expresso in very small cups with large amounts of sugar. *Café Americano* is weaker and served in a larger cup. *Café con leche* is strong black coffee and hot milk.

*Refrescos* or non-alcoholic fruit water-based drinks are found all over. They are a cross between sweetened fruit juice, fruit punch or Kool Aid. *Guarapo* is a juice made from sugar cane. **Tropicola** is the local version of Coke or Pepsi and most widely consumed soft drink. By the way, Coke and Pepsi can sometimes be found here in stores. Fanta or Cuban-made **Najita** is also readily available.

Rum or *ron* is the national drink of Cuba. Both white and dark rum are produced from sugar cane and molasses. Cuba's abundance of tropical fruits are combined with rum to make a variety of exotic cocktails. The famous *daiquiri* is made with light rum and green limes. *Mojito* is a similar drink made with rum, lime juice, sugar and water. The *Piña Colada* (a pineapple based drink) and *Cuba Libre* (rum and coke with a slice of lime) are also favorite drinks. Cuba's bartenders are considered by many to be some of the best in the world.

Beer is another favorite beverage. **Hatuey, Bucanero** and **Cristal** are the best Cuban beers. Mexican and other foreign beers like Heineken are imported. You can also find a few U.S., Mexican and Canadian beers. A number of wines are imported from Spain, South America, France and even California.

Most hotels have bars serving a variety of exotic drinks and offering spectacular views from their top floors. The bars at the **Hotel Ambos Mundos, Hotel Plaza, Hotel Inglaterra** and **Hotel Nacional** should be visited. There are also other bars worth checking out. Try **Papa's** at the Hemingway Marina. The bar-restaurant **La Cecila** famous for its hors d'oeuvres and **El Mirador** bar is a scenic terrace-bar and a good place to view the best sunsets in Havana.

There are two special 'watering holes' deserving special mention. **La Bodeguita del Medio** is famous for its legendary *mojitos* and being a one-time Hemingway haunt. **El Floridita** was another Hemingway hang-out and the birthplace of the *daiquiri*. **The Dos Hermanos Bar** is another place to "wet your whistle."Other cities and towns have less famous but abundant places to have a drink.

# Eating Out

Havana's restaurants serve a variety of cuisine for all tastes and budgets. Most restaurants feature International Cuisine, Caribbean seafood, red meat and Creole dishes. However, many are high priced and geared toward the tourist trade. After you have lived in Cuba for a while you will discover many eateries on you own.

Two types of restaurants exist in Cuba. Government-operated establishments and private restaurants often in converted homes called paladares.

Good restaurants can be found in the majority of hotels. Try either **El Barracón** or **La Sierra Maestra** restaurant—with its spectacular view— in the Havana Libre Hotel. The **Hostal Valencia** hotel serves Spanish food. **Comedor del Hotel Comodoro** specializes in rice dishes. **El Barracón** in the Hotel Havana Libre is one of the city's finest restaurants.

**La Bodeguita del Medio** near the Cathedral, and **La Cecilia**, in the Miramar district, feature typical Cuban food. **El Floridita**, on the corner of Obispo and Monserrate in Old Havana, was a favorite of Hemingway as we mentioned. It is also famous for its seafood dishes like lobster. Besides its drinks, **Papa's Restaurant**, at the Hemingway Marina, specializes in seafood dishes guaranteed to satiate your pallet. **El Pavo Real** (peacock), in Miramar, has the reputation of being Havana's best Chinese Restaurant. **Tocororo** is one of the most famous restaurants in Miramar and known for its shrimp and creole dishes. **The Roof Garden Restaurant** atop the Hotel Sevilla is considered one of Havana's best. **La Paella**, in the Hostal Valencia, offers excellent Spanish food.

Barrio Chino in Central Havana has a number of restaurants serving oriental cuisine.

There are several restaurants which serve different international dishes. **El Patio**, in Old Havana on the Plaza de la Catedral, is worth trying. It is open 24 hours and its prices for some dishes are high. **Las Ruinas**, in Lenin Park, is considered Havana's most exclusive restaurant. It is set in the ruins of an old sugar mill and the ambience is special. The **1830 Restaurant**, in Miramar, also specializes in international dishes. It is set in an elegant bay-side mansion on the sea-side Malecón. **El Cochinito** (The Little Pig), on Calle 23, has criollo food. **La Torre**, at the top of the Focsa building, serves French cuisine and offers a breathtaking, panoramic view of the city and bay.

There are restaurants located in other parts of the country in major resorts, but one deserves special mention because of its setting. **El Castillo de las Nubes** located in the town of Soroa in Pinar del Río Province is definitely worth visiting. It is located on the top of a hill and offers a spectacular panoramic view of the countryside.

# Housing

In Cuba there is a selection of furnished and unfurnished apartments and even houses for rent to foreigners.

As a standard rule of thumb, newcomers to any country should never buy a house, condominium or other property "right off the plane". Only a fool would make such a stupid mistake.

When looking for a place to rent it is always best to shop around and compare prices if you are looking to save money. The first thing you should do is find a hotel or room to use for temporary living while you search for permanent lodging and decide where you want to live. Then search for an apartment or house to rent for at least six months to a year in order to get acquainted with the customs and living conditions and to sample the weather. After this time if you decide that living in Cuba is not for you, you are not burdened with having to get rid of a piece of property.

To find a house or apartment start by talking to other foreigners who live in the area you like. This won't be difficult since a kind of bond exists between foreigners living abroad. You will make good friends easily. They will almost always know someone who is renting or selling property. If you can read

Spanish try looking in the local paper. The prices are usually lower and you can find good deals.

If you don't understand Spanish you should learn the following words so you can understand ads and signs when looking for housing: *agua caliente*-hot water, *alfombrado*-carpeted, *amueblado*-furnished, *sin muebles*- unfurnished, *baño*-bathroom, *cocina*-kitchen, *cochera* or *garaje*-garage, *contrato*-contract, *déposito* or *anticipo*-deposit, *dormitorio*-bedroom, *guarda*-guard, *jardín*-garden, *seguro*-safe, *patio*-patio, *parqueo* or *estacionamiento*-parking.

Talk to people on the street and let them know you are looking to rent. Walk around the neighborhood in your favorite area, ask questions and look for signs that say *"Se alquila "* which means "for rent". When you do find a house or apartment to rent, try using a native Spanish speaker to approach the owner and ask what the price is. This way you can find out what the real price is and not be taken advantage of because you are a foreigner. In most Latin American countries there is a two-tiered price system: inflated prices for tourists and real prices for residents. Knowing this can save you money in the long run.

When you do find a rental, before handing over any money or signing a rental agreement be sure to see if: there is a hot water tank and it works, all the faucets and valves work and there is adequate water pressure, all the toilets function properly, the water is potable; the light switches and plugs work, each room has enough outlets, the house or apartment has a phone, the roof leaks—very important during the rainy season, there is garbage service available; there are signs of cockroaches, other bugs or rats, all of the locks, doors and windows work correctly, the house is secure against robberies, there is enough closet space, there is mail delivery, there is a bus stop, market, hospital and school nearby—if you have children. Air conditioning is necessary. Are pets permitted? Are there noisy neighbors and heavy traffic?

Even if you you are renting on a month-to-month basis, you should make sure your house or apartment meets most of the above conditions. If you do decide to sign a lease or contract, make sure you know what you are signing. Have your lawyer or some other knowledgeable person check all the papers. Have a copy translated for yourself. Ask for lower rent if you sign a long-term deal. Also make sure the owner will take care of repairs and provide security. A live-in maid or gardner can help watch your place when you are away.

If you decide you want to remain in Cuba and choose to buy property, be sure and follow the same procedure as we suggested above when renting property. If everything meets with your satisfaction, you are almost ready to buy. However, first check to see if the person who is selling you the property is really the owner. In Latin America it is common practice for someone who is not the owner to sell a piece of property. Another scam is to sell the same property to several different people. Check all public records like the title of the land and see if there are encumbrances or taxes owed. Whatever you do don't buy anything 'sight unseen', however tempting it may seem. Don't be an impulsive buyer.

When buying don't forget to compare prices in the area to make sure you are getting a good deal and not paying too much. Also find out about taxes, transfer costs and other fees. Finally, go to a reliable lawyer and have all the paperwork checked before any money is exchanged or anything is signed. We have heard too many horror stories of foreigners being swindled in real estate ventures in other Latin American countries.

So, do your homework and be careful! It is also advisable to talk with other foreigners who have purchased real estate. Find out what obstacles they have encountered. Be sure to ask them for advice and any other helpful information they are willing to provide. This is especially true if you decide to build a home. By doing your home work you can save yourself a lot of grief and unnecessary errors in the long run.

If you do build a home someday, don't expect things to go as smoothly as you planned. Things work differently in the third world. Make allowances for untimely delays, the work ethic of your laborers, bureaucracy, and the availability of certain building material

# Lodging

Cuba currently has about 180 hotels and 30,000 rooms available. In this section there is a partial list of hotels you may use for temporary lodging while you look for a house, apartment or some other type of accommodations. A couple of the hotels are very expensive but have been included anyway. If you take your time and look around you will find more reasonably priced lodging. In some cases, you may even be able to rent a room from a family. Your lifestyle and resources really determine what type of living facilities you end up with. Since you will probably be using Havana as a starting point or home base, hotels in other parts of the country are listed in the back of this book.

**Ambos Mundos** is moderately priced on Obispo 153 between San Ignacio and Mercaderes. Tel: 66-9530, Fax: 66-9532.

**Bruzón** is another inexpensive place to stay for cost-conscious travellers. It is on Bruzón Street near the Plaza de la Revolutión. Tel: 57 - 5684.

**Capri** is upscale and located on N Street and Mar Street located in the Vedado district. Tel: 33-3747, Fax: 33-3750.

**Caribbean** is famous with travellers on a budget. It is on Prado 164 at the corner of Calle Colón in Central Havana. Tel 33-8233 Fax: 62-2071.

**Colinas** is moderately priced on L Street Avenue 27 in Vedado Tel: 33 - 4071, Fax: 33 - 4104.

**Comodoro** on Avenida 1ra and Calle 84 is upscale and has good sports facilities. It is in Miramar at 84th Street and Avenue 1 Tel: 24 - 5551, Fax: 24 - 2028.

**Deauville Hotel** is moderately priced on Avenue Italia between Malecón and San Larzo. Centrally located with a roof- top pool and nightclub. Tel: 33 - 8812, Fax: 33 - 8148.

**Havana Libre** is a deluxe hotel on L Street and 23 Street in Vedado. Formerly called the Havana Hilton it has 600 rooms with balconies, a cabaret and post office. Tel: 33 - 4011, Fax: 33 - 3141.

**Havana Riviera Malecón** and Paseo in Vedado. One of the most exclusive and luxurious hotels in Havana. It has two bars and a cabaret. Tel: 33 - 4051, Fax: 33-3739.

**Hotel Plaza** Zulueta and Neptuno. It is an upscale turn-of-the-century hotel located in Old Havana. Tel: 33 - 8583, Fax: 33-8869.

**Hotel Presidente** is an art deco-style establishment and considered by many travelers to be over priced. Calzada and G in Vedado district near the Malecón. Tel: 33 - 4074.

**Hostal Valencia** Oficios Street #53, corner Obrapia and Lamparilla in Old Havana. Tel: 57 -1037 Fax: 33-5628.

**Inglaterra** is in the midprice range on Paseo del Prado #416 between San Rafael and Neptuno in Havana Vieja. Tel: 33 - 8993, 62-7071, Fax: 33 - 8254.

**Lido Consulado** Street near the corner of Animas in Central Havana. Cheap rates. Tel: 57 - 1102, Fax: 33 - 8814.

**Lincoln** is low priced on Galiano and Virtudes Streets. Tel: 33 - 8209.

**Meliá Cohiba** Paseo between 1st and 3rd in Vedado, is Havana's newest luxury hotel. Tel: 24 - 3636, Fax: 33 -3939.

**Morro Hotel** is overpriced on D Street. Tel: 33 - 3907..

**Nacional** O Street and 21 Street in Vedado. Is a deluxe hotel famous for its magnificent view of Havana. It also has a cabaret and good pharmacy. Tel: (07) 33-3564 Fax: 33-5054.

**Sevilla** is definitely upscale on Trocadero #55 between Zulueta and Prado in Old Havana. Tel: 33-8560 fax: 33 - 8582.

**St. John's Hotel** is reasonably priced on O Street, between 23 Street and 25 Street in Vedado. Nightclub, cabaret. and roof-top pool Tel: 33 - 3740, Fax: 33 - 3361.

**Triton** is mid-range on 70 Street and Mar Street in Miramar. Tel: 33-1483 Fax: 33-0042.

**Vedado** next to St. John's Hotel and similarly priced on O Street, # 244, between 23 and 25 Streets in the Vedado neighborhood. Tel: 33 - 4062..

**Victoria** is a deluxe hotel built in the 1920's on 19 Street, # 101, corner of M Street in Vedado. Tel: 33 - 3510, Fax: 33 - 3109.

# Health Care

Cuba is a healthy country and is famous for having the best heath care system in Latin America. Many developed countries lag behind Cuba in medical care. All medical care is free. Birth is a natural event, taken for granted in most developed nations. But, for millions elsewhere, it can be a fearful and dangerous experience. Cuba has one of the lowest infant mortality rates in the world of 7.2 per 1000 live births—almost as low as the U.S. and Canada. In Latin America only Argentina, Chile, Uruguay and Costa Rica have the same low levels of infant mortality as Cuba.

With a life expectancy rate of 75, Cuba also ranks with the U.S. and other developed countries. Health care personnel are found in both urban and rural areas. Hospitals are well equipped. There are about 270 hospitals and 422 poly clinics (half hospital/half clinic) all over the country. Every village has a medical facility. Cuban doctors are considered experts in some areas of research and experimentation. Cuba has around 60,000 doctors (about one for every 250 persons) which is one of the highest ratios in the world and about twice as many per capita as in the U.S.

First-rate medical services are available to foreigners, however unlike Cubans they must pay. The cost of medical treatment for foreigners is very reasonable, around $25 per visit. The **Cira García Clinic** (Ave. 20 between Ave. 41 and 19-A, Tel: 26811, 24493) in Havana's Miramar area, cares for foreigners and fills prescriptions. There is no limit to the wide range of medical services available.

Most tourist hotels and resorts have doctors on call and a pharmacy. These pharmacies tend to be better stocked than local ones. However, if you need medicine you can also go to a local pharmacy. Every city and town has an all-night pharmacy or *farmacia*. **Drogería Sarrá** and **Drogería Johnson** are located in Old

Havana. In Centro Havana there is a pharmacy behind the Hotel Inglaterra. In Vedado there is a pharmacy at Calle 23 at M.

**Servimed** operates special clinics for foreigners with fluent English-speaking doctors. If you speak Spanish you may go to any of the local health care centers called **polyclinics** which also provide care for foreigners. In general, the cost of medical care is much lower than in the U.S. For additional information about health services contact Health Tourism, Apartado 16046, Habana, Cuba, Tel: 225511 or 221623, Fax: 202350.

**Hospital Nacional Hermanos Ameijeiras** (Tel: 33-5361 Fax: 33-5036) just off the Malecón in Central Havana specializes in plastic surgery and other cosmetic procedures for foreigners.

Dental care is inexpensive and good but lags behind the U.S., Canada and Europe. The country also has about 10,000 dentists. There is a dentist for about every 1,200 inhabitants.

If you do feel more comfortable having American doctors treat you, then you will have to go to Miami for treatment. This will be one of the advantages to living so near the United States. Obviously if you seek emergency care you have no other choice but to be treated in Cuba.

U.S. Medicare will not provide coverage outside the United States. It is therefore advisable to have some type of health insurance that covers emergency medical care, hospitalization and all eventualities abroad. Check with your insurance company to see what type of coverage they provide for policy holders who reside abroad. Some American companies provide traveller's insurance, but it is not cheap. So far as we know, presently there is no health insurance available for foreign residents of Cuba.

If you are not used to living in a tropical climate, give yourself time to adjust. The most common health problem is taking too much sun You should really limit your time in the sun until you become acclimated. Between May and October, the risk of sunburn is high. use sunscreen, avoid prolonged exposure between 10 am and 4 pm and drink plenty of liquids. Dehydration can pose a problem for those people who are not acclimated to living in a tropical climate. It is also a good idea to have all of your vaccinations up-to date. The water is safe to drink in most of Cuba's cities. You should boil water in the countryside. Drink lots of water so as to not become dehydrated.

Whatever you do, you should try to evaluate your future health care needs to see if they will be taken care of abroad. If you become infirm, it is comforting to know you can hire a servant to do all of your daily tasks for far less than in the U.S. or Canada. So, elderly persons need not worry about finding someone to take care of them.

# Safety

Compared to most Latin American countries, the amount of crime in Cuba is low. In fact the crime rate is less than in any other Latin American or Caribbean country, making Cuba the safest country in the area. There is some petty theft but the type of violent crime found in the U.S. is virtually nonexistent. You will probably feel safer in Cuba than in your home country. Violent crime against foreigners is a rare occurrence. Most of Cubans are honest hard working people.

Unfortunately, Americans, Canadians and Europeans are viewed as millionaires by the people of third world countries, including Cuba. Comparatively speaking we are much better off. There are always a few dishonest individuals looking to take advantage of foreigners. However, if you are alert, exercise common sense and take some basic precautions, you should have few problems with crime in Cuba—better safe than sorry.

Robbery is most likely to take place in large towns and cities. Parts of Havana should be avoided at night. Be especially careful in those areas which have poor lighting and narrow streets.

Pickpockets can be a problem anywhere in the world. So, don't carry large amounts of your money, your passport or valuables in exposed areas of your clothing. If you have to carry large amounts money, conceal it with a money belt or another device underneath your clothes. Keep a small amount of money in your pockets to fool would be thieves by making them think that is all you are carrying.

Don't carry original documents. It is advisable to make photocopies of these important papers. Exercise similar precautions to avoid having your purse or camera snatched. Whatever you do, don't flaunt your wealth by wearing expensive jewelry in public places. If you really want to keep a low profile and not stand out, dress down and wear clothing like the locals so you don't stick out like a sore thumb.

Try to avoid street hustlers commonly called *jineteros* who will try to sell you anything or offer to change your money. In Havana Vieja there have been a lot of purse snatchings and muggings as in the downtown areas of Cuba's major cities. But most U.S. cities have more crime in a year than in all of Cuba. Women should be careful of men harassing them. This is another form of machismo in a male dominated society. The best thing to do is just ignore these men. They are just flirting and saying flattering but often vulgar remark—called *piropos*.

When exploring the island as a tourist, never leave your things on the beach unattended when going swimming. Don't lose sight of your luggage or leave valuables in your hotel room. Have a safe place in your apartment or house to hide your most prized possessions. However tempting it may appear, don't change money with black market street traders. This practice is illegal, risky and you most often end up getting ripped off in some way. Avoid walking on dark streets and in out of the way places at night.

As for burglary, you are better off living in an apartment or condominium or a single detached dwelling. The former tend to be less susceptible to burglary due to their design and the fact that there is "safety in numbers". Apartments sometimes have intercoms, security access and even guards. Neighbors will usually help keep an eye on your place if you befriend them. Be sure to inform them when you will be away.

One of the best defenses against burglaries is having a housesitter or a live-in maid. If you do hire a maid, ask for references. Be careful to treat your household help well to ensure their loyalty. It is advisable to have a safety deposit box for jewelry or any other small valuable items. Again, in the long run you are better off toning down your materialistic life-style and not making a ostentatious display of your wealth by having a lot of unnecessary luxury items.

Single women living alone should never walk unaccompanied at night. If you do go out in the evening, be sure to take a cab or have a friend come along. Speaking Spanish will often protect you. It is advisable to know some basic phrases in the event of an emergency.

Men should always watch out for prostitutes who often are expert pickpockets. They are also known to work with accomplices who will gang up on unsuspecting victims at a most inopportune moment. Also, never walk alone at night when intoxicated. You are a sitting duck.

Be careful of overly friendly strangers. Treat anyone you meet on the street with caution. Don't put too much trust in new acquaintances. Watch out for people who offer you get rich scams or try to sell you land "sight unseen". If it seems too good to be true, it usually is. White collar crime is a world-wide problem. Don't be naive and think just because you are in a third world country nobody will try to swindle you. You don't have to be paranoid, just be more cautious than normal. If you use your common sense you will avoid most problems.

In the event that you are robbed, accosted or bilked out of money, you should contact the local authorities as soon as possible. If you lose you passport or other documents, contact your local embassy or consulate (see the list included in this book).

## Communications

The Ministry of Communications or *El Ministerio de Comunicaciones* is in charge of the country's post offices and telephone services. There are branches located all over the country. In Havana there is a post and telegraph office conveniently located in the lobby of the Hotel Havana Libre Building 23 and L Streets. Other post offices in Havana can be found at the Estación Central de Ferrocarriles on Avenida Bélgica and Arsenal in Old Havana; at 23 Street at C in Vedado and in the Ministry of Communications building on *Avenida de la Independencia* between *Plaza de la Revolución* and the bus station. Most tourist hotels sell stamps.

In La Havana Vieja, dollar postoffices are at Oficios No. 102 on Plaza de San Francisco de Asís, and in Centro Havana in the Gran Teatro on Paseo de Martí at the Capitolio end of the building.

Besides mailing correspondence, post and telegraph offices offer the following services—fax, telegrams and cables. You can buy stamps (*sellos*) at hotels and post offices (*oficinas de Correos*). In general, postal rates are low. A letter to the U.S. and Canada costs around 65¢, to Europe 75¢, 05¢ within the country, 65¢ to South America and 65¢ to Central America. A postcard costs around 50¢ to all countries.

It is better to send all correspondence from Havana. Mailboxes are blue in Cuba. Just as in the rest of Latin America, postal service is unreliable and slow . Mail from the provinces and other parts of the country takes much longer to reach its overseas destination. Even so, letters can take up to a month to get to some foreign countries. So, it is best to ask a tourist or someone else to mail your correspondence abroad. When mailing from Cuba it is advisable to write the country destination in Spanish to speed things up.

If you are sending parcels you might want to try the international courier service **DHL** (Tel: 33-4543, Fax: 33-5016) for faster service. The main office is in Havana at Aerocaribbean Calle 23 # 64 at "P" in Vedado. They have another office at Calzada No. 818, between Calles 2 and 4, near the Hotel Meliá Cohiba (Tel: 33-4351). There are also branches in other parts of the country. The rates for a letter weighing less than 8 ounces from the U.S. to Cuba are about $70 and from Cuba to the U.S. around $25. It usually takes about four business days for a letter or package to reach Cuba from the U.S. and three business days from Cuba to the U.S. Obviously, if you are going to the U.S. or Canada it is easier to mail your letters or packages from there.

Cuba's telephone system is antiquated and in need of an overhaul. Presently the country only has about 350,000 telephone lines. However, in an effort to modernize the **Cuban Telecommunications Company** (ETECSA) has started to expand service install new digital exchanges in the country's main cities. It is easy to make an international call from a hotel. If you don't have a phone, use the phone and fax office at the Havana Libre or another hotel for long distances or international calls. Some hotels have direct dialing. In Havana, international calls may also be made from the **Minister of Communications** building at the Plaza de la Revolución, 351 Obispo Street. Small cities and towns have telephone offices where both local and long distance calls are made. Within Cuba, calls may be made by dialing O, the the city or area code and local number. Public pay phones are all over the country but can't be used for international calls and service is poor. They accept Cuban coins or *centavos*. Rates are determined by distance. Local rates are 20-50 cents (USD) and long distance within Cuba costs $1.00-$2.00. Long distance cost is $2.50 to

$4.00 per minute to North and Central America and $5.00 to the rest of the world.

To make an international call to the U.S. dial 119 to reach the international operator. Dial 88 and then the country code, the area and number to reach other countries. To place a call through the operator dial 00 for local calls or 09 for international calls. There is a new phone book but it is often difficult to find the number you are looking for. Information is reached by dialing 113. Dial 10 for the local operator, 116 for the police, 115 to report a fire and 118 for an ambulance. To call Cuba from the U.S. or Canada dial your international access code 011 followed by Cuba's country code-53 , the area or city code and the local telephone number in Cuba. You may need the help of an operator.

In the 1990's cellular phone service was introduced to Cuba by a state-run comoany called Cubacel (in a joint venture between Mexican's TIMSA phone company and Emtelcuba). Cubacel will activate your cell phone. Regular monthly service charges are about $40. There is an activation fee and air time is around 50 cents per minute. You should bring your own cell phone with you since they are very expensive in Cuba. Their office in Havana is at the José Martí Airport Tel: (33) 2222 or (33) 1737, website: www.cubacell.com. They also have branches at José Martí International Airport Tel: (80) 0043, in Varadero Tel: 80-9222 and in Santiago de Cuba Tel: 8-6199.

Cubacel also rents cell phones for under $10 per day plus a security deposit. You may make and receive international calls with your rented phone.

**Caribbean Radio Services,** a Panamanian registered company with an office in Havana, provides voice and paging service in Havana and the resort of Varadero. They rent and sell satellite and telephone equipment, telex equipment, facsimile machines and cellular phones.

Telegrams may be sent from post offices. Most hotels and tourist facilities have fax machines for your convenience.

Currently there are more than 1,000 users of the Internet in Cuba. Businesses, organizations and ministries may send and receive E-mail, have websites and access the Internet services. You may receive and send e-mail in Havana at the **Infocom** office in Miramar. They also provides webpage design and software services. You may contact them at: **Oficina Comercial de Elecsa**, Calle 22 e/ 3ra y 5ta, Miramar, Playa, Cuidad de la Habana, Tel: (24) 7036 Fax: (24) 3977 E-mail: infomire@teleda.get.cma.net. or webmaster@mail. infocon.elecsaiw. Cuba's Internet provider, Cenial operates a cybercafe at Havana's Capitolio. The Melía Cohiba, Havana Libre, Hotel Nacional, Golden Tulip, and Meliá Havana all offer full internet access and e-mail for an hourly fee.

Here are some other Cuba Internet and E-mail contacts: www.internetcuba.com, www.cubacan.cu, http://cubana.cu, http://granma.cu and http://www.prensa-latina.org.

If you don't speak Spanish you will have problems making and receiving phone calls, sending faxes and mailing letters. Here are a few key Spanish phrases to help you.

---

*Yo quisiera poner un telegrama/fax* — I would like to send a telegram/fax.

*Yo quisiera hacer una llamada persona a persona* — I would like to make a personal call.

*Yo quisiera hacer una llamada de larga distancia* — I would like to make a long distance call.

*Yo quisiera hacer una llamada de cobro revertido* — Reverse the charges.

*Por favor, comuníqueme con este número* — Please dial/connect me with this number.

---

*La línea está ocupada* — The line is busy.

*aló, hola, diga* — hello

*número equivocado* — wrong number

*Yo quisiera hablar con......* — I would like to speak with......

*No se encuentra....* — so and so is not in.

*Quisiera dejar un recado* — I would like to leave a message.

*marcar* — to dial

*cabina* — phone booth

*moneda* — coin

*el correo, la oficina de correo* — post office

*buzón* — mail box

*estampilla* , sello — stamp

# Transportation

Before you set out to explore Cuba you should realize the country is bigger than it appears on maps—nearly 1000 miles from end to end. The fastest way to get around is by air. **Cubana de Aviación** has inter-island flights connecting Havana with about a dozen main cities including the Island of the Youth. **Aero Caribbean** 79-5224 offers many charter flights and service to those areas not served by Cubana. One way domestic prices range from $20 to $80 depending on your destination.

The **Ministry of Transportation**, or MITRANS, operates all passenger trains. In Cuba train travel is a way to get from one place to another. It also allows you to see some of the sights and countryside along the way. Cuba has around 8000 miles of railway with two-thirds used by the sugar industry and the remaining part for passenger service. The main rail line passes through the center of the country from Pinar del Río Province to Havana to Santiago de Cuba at the other end of the island. There are also several branches off the main line which go to smaller cities and towns. There is an electric train that goes from Havana to the city of Matanzas.

Don't expect to find the same kind of comforts as you do on European and U.S. trains. Cuba's passenger trains are most often slow moving, unclean, have windows that don't open, air conditioning that is too high or too low and schedules that are unreliable. Despite these shortcomings, if you do travel by train, choose first class since air conditioning is usually available. The overnight express from Havana to Santiago offers fairly good service. The 600 mile trip takes about 16 hours and the train passes through through many cites along the way. This is the best way to meet Cubans and see the country.

In Havana tickets may be purchased in advance at the Ladis (formerly known as Ferotour office) Tel; (62) 4259 behind the Central Railway Station or Estación Central de Ferrocarril in Habana Vieja Tel: (5702041. In Santiago de Cuba at the other end of the rail line, call Ferrotour at (07) 22254 to make reservations.

Cuba has about 10,000 miles of paved roads and boasts of one of the best road systems in Latin America. The main highway—*La Carretera Central* or Central Highway—goes almost from one end of the island to the other running from Pinar del Río in the west to Santiago for a total length of over 800 miles. There is also an eight-lane expressway linking only part of the island. It extends from Pinar del Río to just east of Santa Clara.

Other highway is the one that comes from Havana to Varadero and joins the cays around Cayo Guillermo and callo Coco. In addition to the paved highways, there are a number of small or secondary roads which traverse the country at various points and unpaved "farm-to-market-roads". Many roads are unpaved and full of pot holes.

When driving in the countryside, only drive during the day. Be sure to watch out for livestock, pedestians and bicycles. Also, remember to take along some type of map and be careful of blind curves when travelling in mountainous areas. During the rainy season improved roads can turn into quagmires. Try not to venture off the main paved road or you will run the risk of getting stuck in the mud and possibly stranded in a remote area. To drive legally in the country you must be 21 years old and have either an International Driver's License or a national driver's license.

Buses are the backbone of Cuba's public transportation system. Almost everyone depends on the bus system for travel within and between cities. Cuban buses or gua-guas (wha-whas) are used in cities and towns for local travel. In the capital a type of tractor-trailer buses known as camellos are used. All that is required is having the patience to stand in long lines to use this form of transportation. For long distance travel there are air conditioned interprovincial tourist buses. Many of these buses are newer European models. They go to and from Havana and service most of the country. There are also smaller, less comfortable buses with no air conditioning that travel frequently between the majority of the cities and towns.

Bus travel is usually inexpensive and quicker than travelling by train. Be sure to make your reservations in advance, especially during the peak tourist season, weekends or holidays. All major cities and most towns have bus terminals. **Havanatour** Tel: 33-2712 Fax: 33-2601 and other companies offer modern air conditioned bus service to resort areas.

**Havauotos** (main office Calle 36, No. 505, Av. 5e, Miramar, Havana, Tel:23-9815), www.havanaautos.cubaweb.cu , **Cubanacán** (Tel:33-0742), **National Rent-a-car** (Tel: 81-0357 Fax: 33-0742) and **Transautos** (Tel: 24-5532 Fax: 24-4057) are agencies offering car rentals. **CUBACAR** which has offices in Havana, Varadero and five other locations offers car rentals over the Internet. You may contact them at: E-mail cubacar@cbcan.cyt..cu or by phone at (537) 24-2718 or fax them at (537) 33-0760. You must be at least 21 years old and posses either an International Driver's License or a valid national driver's license to drive. There are also individuals who have their own cars and work as private chauffeurs. They will be glad to take you to your destination or show you the sights.

Havana has plenty of taxis for tourists, businessmen and foreign residents. Taxis may be found around most hotels and in other areas of Cuba's cities. To get a taxi in Havana call 81-0153, 35-5539 or 33-6312. **Turistax** and **Panataxi** are larger companies. But here are also numerous licensed and unlicensed private taxis. Some taxis cater exclusively to tourists. Other ordinary taxis are used by anyone who can afford this mode of transportation. Special long-distance taxis can be booked through **Infotur** (Palace del Turismo, Calle Obispo, Havana, Tel:61-1544).

## Finding Your Way Around

In Cuba most addresses are given as locations and street numbers are occasionally used. For example, in Havana the address of a building, business, restaurant, hotel or home may be described as between two streets on a certain avenue, then followed by the neighborhood or district . Streets (*calles*) and avenues (*avenidas*) are almost laid out on the old Spanish rectangular grid system centered at a main square or plaza with parallel streets (*calles*) running perpendicular to avenues (*avenidas*). Some towns have even numbered streets running perpendicular to odd-numbered streets. An address may also be given as being on the corner (*esquina* or esq.) or between (*entre*, or e/) cross street.

However, be aware that many streets have changed names but continue to be known by their old names. This practice of double-naming is common. Below is a list of both the new and old names (in parenthesis) of the main streets in Havana.

Argamonte (Zulueta)

Avenida Carlos Manuel de Cespedes (Avenida del Puerto)

Avenida de España (Vives)

Avenida de Italia (Galiano)

Avenida de la Independencia (Avenida de Rancho Boyeros)

Avenida de las Misiones (Monserrate)

Avenida México (Cristina)

Avenida Salvador Allende (Carlos III)

Avenida Simón Bolívar (Reina)

Brasil (Teniente Rey)

Calle 23 (La Rampa)

Calle G (Avenida de los presidentes)

Enrique barnet (Estrella)

Leonor Pérez (Paula)

Malecón (Avenida Maceo)

Máximo Gómez (Monte)

Padre Varela (Belascoaín)

Paseo de Martí (Paseo del prado)

San Martín (San José)

On the last page of this book we have included a table with the approximate distance between many points within the country. It should help you find your way around if you travel by car. Due to a lack of space we couldn't possibly include all of the cities, larger towns or beach resorts.

# (UBANS S(ENES

There is always time for fun in Cuba.

Cuba's spectacular countryside.

Havana's water front in the distance.

Many of the locals use bicycles to get around.

Cuba is a sportsfisheman's paradise.

One of Cuba's movie theaters.

La Floridita, one
Hemingway's old
haunts, is still open to
the public.

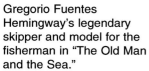

Hemingway's boat,
"El Pilar."

Gregorio Fuentes
Hemingway's legendary
skipper and model for the
fisherman in "The Old Man
and the Sea."

A stately mansion reflects Cuba's past splendor.

The Capitolio is modeled after the U.S. capital.

Monuments reflect Cuba's colorful history.

Vintage cars abound in Cuba.

An example of colonial architecture.

The seaside Malecón is the ideal place for people watching.

José Martí Airport is the gateway to Cuba.

Baseball is Cuba´s most popular sport. Cuba´s famous pitcher, "El Duque", shows his stuff.

A Havana street scene.

# CHAPTER 7

## SAVING MONEY

### Living for Less Abroad

Depending on your lifestyle you should be able to live for considerably less than in the U.S., Canada or Europe. Food, housing, transportation and most entertainment are cheaper and you will not have huge winter heating bills. One of the best ways to figure out if you can afford to live in Cuba is to compare your income with the wages of the workers of the country. This gives an accurate picture of your purchasing power and tells you how much you probably need to maintain your current lifestyle. But you must not assume professionals and others earn as much as their counterparts in the U.S., Canada or Europe. A social security check of a thousand dollars a month will enable you to live far better than most professionals in the majority of Latin American countries not, to mention Cuba.

The majority of Americans and Canadians will be able to have a maid, gardener, go out to eat and drink most evenings, afford entertainment, buy clothing and food and, in general, enjoy a lifestyle as good if not better that they would at home.

Another factor making Cuba affordable is the two-tiered price system. It is one thing to visit Cuba as a tourist and another to live there. Tourists stay in high-priced hotels, eat their meals in restaurants and generally live "high on the hog" by paying "top dollar" for everything. On the other hand, as a resident, you will save money by renting, purchasing food in markets and spending less. You will also learn to bargain or haggle for prices as done in the rest of Latin America.

However, the real secret to a low cost of living and getting more for your money is to try to "live like them locals." This does not mean you have to live in abject poverty but learn to economize in many situations.

---

## Cost of Living

Approximate Monthly Cost of Living and Prices as of June 1998

Apartment (small, 1-2 bedrooms)............................................$200
House (small) ......................................................................$250+
Electric Bill (apt.) ................................................................$3.00
Telephone(basic rate) ..........................................................$3.00
Telephone Calls: Local (3min.) 5 centavos; Long Distance within Cuba Sliding scale according to distance; Long Distance U.S. $2.50per minute; Americas $4.00 per minute; Europe $5.50 per minute
Tips   10-15%
Taxi   $1.00 per kilometer plus 20% at night
Local bus fare ..................standard fare 10 centavos to one peso
Gasoline ...............(regular) $.65 per liter; (super) $1.10 per liter
Minimum wage........... ($6 to $12 monthly as stipulated by the government)
Restaurant (inexpensive)............................................$3.00 - $10.00
Restaurant (hotel) .....................................................$4.00 - $12.00
Beer . .........................................................................$.75 - $2.00
Coffee (small cup)........................................................20 centavos
Doctor's visit............................................................$25.00 - $35.00
Air Mail letter ..................$.65 U.S.; $.45 Americas; $.75 Europe
**\*These prices are subject to fluctuations at any time**

---

When figuring out your projected living expenses before considering a move abroad, be sure to take into account the following factors: currency variations, the relative cost and availability of consumer items, the price of entertainment, housing prices, utilities (water, garbage, electricity and telephone) and health care. You should also consider the cost of a vehicle, registration, fuel, maintenance and insurance. be sure and also factor in airfare to and from the country.

High import taxes are a way of life in almost all Latin American countries. Therefore, you will be better off buying domestic goods, if possible. Before you bring anything from abroad be sure and find out how much duty you'll have to pay.

Once you have lived in Cuba for a while, learned all of the-ins-and-outs, studied the advice in this book and made contacts, you will be able to cut your living costs substantially. This is important for those people living on small or fixed incomes.

You might want to invest, start a small business, share a home or apartment, work as a consultant if you have a particular field of expertise, trade your services or engage in other money making ventures to further reduce your living expenses. With a little creativity and imagination you will be able to find you niche and save money in the process.

## Money

Up to 1934, when peso bills were first introduced, the US dollar was Cuba's only type of currency, . Currently there are three types of currency in Cuba: the **Cuban peso**, the convertible peso and the US dollar.

The peso is Cuba's official monetary unit. It is divided into 100 centavos or cents. Currently there is an official exchange rate of 1 peso to 1 dollar but its actual value is around 20 to one. The following bills are in circulation at the present time in Cuba:

1 *peso*, 3 *pesos*, 5 *pesos*, 10 *pesos*, 20 *pesos* and 50 *pesos*. The most common coins, or *monedas*, are: 1 *peso*, 40 *centavos*, 20 *centavos*, 10 *centavos* and 5 *centavos* 2 and 1 *centavos*. It is a good idea to have a supply of 5 *centavo* coins if you plan to use buses or pay phones or to buy food.

In 1994 the convertible peso was introduced. Since it has the same value as the US dollar and the latter are more widely accepted, it is more advantageous to use dollars than *pesos*.

The US dollar, for all practical purposes, has become the currency of Cuba. Increasingly the US dollar is being used for transactions. It is estimated that around 50% of the Cuban population uses the US dollar. Tourists will have to pay for all transactions in dollars since the peso is basically worthless. Most resort facilities, hotels, restaurants and other places dealing with foreigners will only accept dollars. Currently, only non-U.S. credit cards and traveler's checks are accepted.US-issued credit cards won't be accepted. Someday this will all change when relations between the US and Cuba are normal. **Banco Financiero** will cash American Express traveller's checks.

You may get a cash advance and change money at the **Banco Financiero Internacional** in the Havana Libre Hotel in Vedado. Cash may also be obtained from ATMS all around Havana. However, at present they aren't set up to accept Visa or MasterCard.If you desire information about what credit cards are accepted in Cuba go to the **Centro de Tarjetas de Crédito** at 23rd Street by the Havana Libre Hotel, Vedado Tel: 33-4444 Fax: 33-4001. Traveller's checks are accepted and may be cashed at most hotels but you have to pay a 2% to 4% commission.

The **Banco Nacional Central de Cuba** (BCC) has authority over national and foreign banks. Money can be changed at the National Bank of Cuba or **Banco Nacional de Cuba**. It is state run and the country's main commercial bank. Over 150 branch offices can be found throughout the country. It is open weekdays from around 8:30 a.m. - 3 p.m. The main branch in Havana is at Cuba

402, corner of Lamparilla, Tel: (7)-62-5361. To avoid delays and long waits it is faster to change money at tourist hotels. In 1995 the government let Cubans open interest-bearing savings accounts and certificates of deposits. Loans are now available for the self employed. In addition, Cuban banks now offer travelers checks, money transfers, checking accounts and other services to Cuban and foreign businesses, Cuban citizens, joint ventures and foreign residents.

**Banco Internacional de Comercio** or **Bicsa**, works with foreign correpondent banks and opens foreign currency accounts for foreginers and foreign entities.

Opening a bank account can be complicated in Cuba. We advise you to check with one of the banks listed below for their requirements.

Here is a list of Cuban Banks:

---

**Banco Nacional de Cuba** (Banco de Crédito y Comercio)
  Aguiar No. 411 e/Amargura Y lamparilla, Habana Vieja
(Old Havana).
Tel: (53-7) 66-6660 and 66-6661
Fax: (53-7) 66-9390

**Banco Central de Cuba**
Cuba No. 402, Habana, Vieja (Old Havana)
Tel: (53-7) 33-8003 and 62-7601
Fax: (53-7) 66-6601

**Banco Internacional de Comercio, S.A.**
20 de mayo y Ayestarán, Plaza, Ciudad de Habana
Tel: (53-7) 33-5115
Fax: (53-7) 33-5112

---

**Banco Financiero Internacional**
Línea y O, Vedado
Tel: (53-7) 33-3003
Fax: (53-7) 33-32-3248 or 33-3006
Open Monday through Saturday 8 a.m. - 3 p.m.

**Banco Metropolitano, S.A.**
Línea y M, Vedado
Tel: (53-7) 32-9894 or 55-3116
Fax; (53-7) 33-4241

Presently there are a few foreign banks which may
operate representative offices in Cuba. They mainly cater
to foreign businesses. Here are a couple of contacts.

**ING Bank (Holland)**
Miramar
Tel: (53-7) 24-0419 or 24-0420
Fax: (53-7) 33-8919

**Neederlands Caribbean Bank**
Miramar
Tel: (53-7) 24-0419
Fax: (53-7) 24-0472
Open Monday through Friday 8 a.m. -5 p.m.

As part of a joint venture Mexico's Banamex has permission
to issue credit cards in Cuba. For money transfers try the **Western
Union** office in Havana at Calle Obispo 335, Tel: 62-5297.

Money may also be changed on the black market or mercado
negro. The black market plays an important role in Cuba's
economy. Many imported consumer items of all prices and types
may be purchased on the black market. Be forewarned that
dealing on the black market can be risky and is illegal. You run

the risk of being caught and fined and even ripped off. However, changing money on the black market is a widespread practice.

Tipping used to be illegal, but now is widespread and recommended for good service. Standard tips range from 10% to 15% depending on the quality of service. Employees will also appreciate American-made goods in lieu of money for their services. Taxi drivers always expect to be tipped. Tour guides, waiters, guards who watch your car, maids or anyone who does you a favor beyond the usual call of duty expect to be tipped by foreigners. Service charges or taxes may or may not be included as part of the bill at restaurants.

Be careful, some may try to take advantage of foreigners. You should be familiar with standard rates to avoid getting gypped. It is best to talk to other expats to see when and how much to tip. Foreigners often over tip leading people to expect more for their services and feeling disappointed when you don't give them the usual amount. In the rest of Latin America you may sometimes bribe someone for special services. This practice is not widespread in Cuba and is highly discouraged.

## Expatriates and Taxes

Whatever your nationality, you should be aware of your tax responsibility to your mother country. US citizens living abroad are not exempted from their tax obligations. You may be subject to income tax on any income generated inside Cuba. The present rule states that you may claim a tax exemption up to $80,000 on "foreign-earned income" if you are a resident of another country and live outside of the country for 330 days in a 365 day period. If you reside outside of the U.S. you may wait to file your taxes until June 15th. If you have questions contact **IRS International** in Washington, DC at 202-874-1460 or their Mexico City office at 905-211-0042. See their Publication 54, Tax Guide for U.S. Citizens and Resident Aliens Abroad.

You may also want to pick up a copy of the *Expats Guide to U.S. Taxes*. It is available through Amazon.com. You can obtain forms and information by using the Internet at: www.ustreas.gov.

At the end of 1996 the Cuban government established the **National Office of Tax Administration** to tax the self employed. Recent tax laws were passed to distribute the country's national income more equitably. New taxes were introduced gradually.

Foreigners who operate joint ventures can take advantage of several tax incentives and tax deferment programs. However, most foreginers who spend more than 180 days in Cuba yearly must pay Cuban income tax.

It must be noted that private Cuban entrepreneurs are taxed heavily in order to protect state enterprises.

If you are interested in reading about the many of tax advantages afforded US citizens residing abroad, we suggest you read Roger Gallo's "*Escape From America*." It is packed full of practical information about the new world economy for the expat.

We also suggest you pick up a copy of Charles Freeman's, "*The Freedom Handbook*". Much like Mr. Gallo's guide it contains insider information for anyone contemplating moving outside of the United States or Canada. Please see our Suggested reading section to order either one of these "must read" books.

You may also want to think of forming a **Panamanian Corporation** to protect your assets while living as an expatriate and while doing business in Cuba. These entities afford the maximum global protection of your assets while living in the US or abroad. Please see the article by the C.P.A. in this section for more details.

For more information on this subject contact: Relocation and Retirement Consultants, Suite 1 SJO 981, P.O. Box 025216, Miami, Fl. 33102, Fax: 011-506-261-8968, E-mail: crbooks@racsa.co.cr

## Panamanian Corporations

Offshore corporations enable you to act as an international citizen with complete confidentiality, privacy and safety. Offshore corporations can legally open offshore bank accounts, brokerage accounts, hold credit cards, own property, stocks, etc. and in many cases completely exempt you from any tax reporting requirements and with complete confidentiality.

### WHY PANAMA?

For many years Panama has been recognized worldwide as a major international offshore banking center offering very attractive legal and tax incentives to Panamanian corporations. For example, Panamanian law allows Panamanian corporations to issue "bearer" stock certificates. This means the owners who control the corporation do not have to be named in any public record, since ownership is through physical possession of the "bearer" shares. Panamanian Corporations are not subject to Panamanian tax on income earned outside of Panama. Also, Panama allows you to name your corporation with an English name, which has many advantages when using your Panamanian Corporation in English speaking countries. These are just a few of the more important reasons why Panamanian corporations are so popular.

### FORMING A PANAMANIAN CORPORATION:

First we recommend you select a name in English followed by: Corp., Corporation, Inc. or Incorporated. You cannot use the words Bank, Trust, Foundation or Insurance in the name of your corporation. You may use any name as long as it is not being currently used in Panama. If you own a US Corporation, you may find some advantages in using the same name for your Panamanian corporation, if available in Panama. This would allow you to have identically named offshore and onshore bank accounts as well as other similar advantages.

Panamanian corporations are typically formed with nominee directors, president, secretary and treasure. These are Panamanian citizens who are modestly paid office workers. If you wish, you may select your own directors and officers. However, the original directors and officers selected are registered with the Panamanian public registry which becomes public information available to anyone who inquires. Therefore, if you wish confidentiality, we recommend you select the nominee director option. Officers and directors can always be changed later.

Panamanian law allows corporate shares to be issued in "bearer" form. This means that whoever physically possesses the shares owns the company. This allows for total confidentiality of ownership, since the person who physically possesses the shares is not identified in any public or even private record. Having a Panamanian corporation with "bearer" shares also makes transfer of ownership completely private and not a matter of public record, since transfer of ownership is a simple process of physically transferring the "bearer" shares to a new owner. It is very similar to passing a $20 bill to someone else versus writing them a check. This feature makes it very easy to sell or transfer properties confidentially by simply transferring the "bearer" shares and ownership of the Panamanian corporation, and thus avoiding many forms of taxes and closing costs because title to the property remains in the name of the Panamanian corporation. Essentially you are simply selling the corporation which owns the property.

Your Panamanian Corporation comes with a notarized General Power of Attorney (in English) signed by two officers named in the articles of incorporation. This power of attorney provides a blank space for you to fill in the name of any person

you want to act as the legal agent for the corporation with the authority to open and sign on corporate bank accounts, enter into contracts for the corporation, sign and transfer assets for the corporation, etc. Although you fill in your name or another person name as having Power of Attorney, this is not evidence of ownership. The person named is simply an agent, similar to an employee empowered to act for the corporation. You may order as many additional Power of Attorney forms as you wish.

As you can see there is a world market for Panamanian corporations because they are extremely popular. Older Panamanian corporations with established bank accounts sell for thousands of dollars or more. Selling your Panamanian corporation is a matter of physically transferring the "bearer" stock certificate together with the other corporate records to the new owner.

The one-time cost for setting up a simple Panamanian Corporation is around $1500. You will have to pay an annual Registered Agent and Director's fee of $500 , due one month before the anniversary date of the corporation.

For additional information about starting a Panamanian corporation contact: **Relocation and Retirement Consultants,** Suite 1 SJO 981, P.O. Box 025116, Miami, Fl 33102-5216 Fax: 011-506-2618968 oe E-mail: panamaniancorps@hotmail.com.

## Insurance

There are several types of insurance available in Cuba. If you have any questions contact the following agencies:

**Seguros Internacionales de Cuba**—(ESICUBA) is Cuba's largest insurance company: Calle Cuba 314, e/Obispo y Obrapia, Havana; Tel: (57) 3231, Fax: 33-8038 offers travellers' insurance (Seguro de Viajero) and other types of coverage except life. They also provide long-term health coverage for foreigners.

**Empresa del Seguro Estatal Nacional**—(ESEN): Avenida 5ta #306, Vedado, Tel: (32) 2508, Fax: (33) 8717. They also have medical insurance for foreign travelers. If you have your own vehicle, you may insure it through them.

**Agencia Internacional de Inspección y Ajuste de Averías y Servicios Conexos**—INTERMAR S.A. : Obispo No 361 between Habana and Compostela, Havana, controls the inspection of goods and breakage, Lloyd's of London: Calle B # 310 between 13 and 15 in Vedado, Tel: 33-4663, Fax: 33-3837.

# CHAPTER 8

## MAKING MONEY
### Cuba's Investment Climate

Before talking about investment opportunities, let's take a brief look at Cuba's economy to get an overall picture of what is happening there. This will help you better understand the investment climate of the country.

Until recently sugar had always been the mainstay of the Cuban economy. At one time sugar accounted for 70% of the country's export revenue. The *zafra* is the sugar cane harvest and runs from November through May. The country produces around 10 million tons of sugar a year. Tobacco has traditionally been the second most important agricultural product. Cuba's Vuelta Abajo region is the best place in the world to grow tobacco for cigars. Cuba's soil and climate are also perfect for growing good coffee. Rice, corn and tropical fruits are other important crops. In general, agriculture has been diversified to feed a burgeoning population.

Cuba has a large reserve of minerals that are exported-especially nickel. About 40% of the world's nickel reserves are found in Cuba and the country is the fourth largest producer in the world. Nickel has traditionally been Cuba's second foreign exchange earner. However, most of the country's minerals have yet to be exploited. Cobalt, copper and iron are other minerals found on the island.

After sugar and nickel, fishing is the country's third most important industry. Cuba's pharmaceutical industry is growing fast and will possibly be an increased source of exports. However, most industry in Cuba basically exists for the production of products for domestic consumption.

At the present time more and more countries, companies and individuals are making profitable investments in Cuba. The second Cuban Revolution in the last fifty years has begun except this one is capitalistic and not communist. This revolution is akin to what is happening in Russia, Vietnam and China. What we are presently seeing are economic reforms preceding political reforms. Cuba cannot afford to not participate in the mainstream of the global economy. Free market ideas are beginning to take root in Cuba.

Over fifty foreign countries are currently doing business in Cuba. Bilateral trade between Cuba and the U.S. will increase in the future. Cuba is so ripe for doing business that many U.S. corporations who had property confiscated in Cuba are probably willing to relinquish claims to what they previously owned just for the chance to "get their foot in the door". Rumor has it that many deals have already been cut behind the scenes. In fact, more than 2,500 U.S. business executives and representatives visited Cuba in 1998.

A number of factors make investments in Cuba attractive. First, its geographic position and proximity to the United States. Someday you will be able commute to Cuba if necessary. Cuba is accessible from all parts of the world by air or sea. A communications system, which includes phone, fax and telex services, links Cuba to the rest of the world. A stable political situation, low level of corruption, signs of economic recovery, a banking system, mass communication (radio T.V. and phones), a postal system, international courier systems, international airports, public transportation, a highly educated work force, unspoiled beaches and other tourists locations, hotels, resorts and a rail and road network all combine to make up a well entrenched infrastructure necessary for foreign investment.

Another important factor to consider is that workers' wages are low when compared to other countries due to Cuba's low wage scale. Cubans who are employed by the government or in joint ventures earn only about $10 monthly. However, there are a lot of people earning more under the table.

Combine these factors with the country's natural beauty and good weather and you have a land ripe for investment. Since Cuba has been isolated from the capitalist mainstream for such a long time, the country is virgin for many business opportunities. Enterprising foreigners will have the chance to start previously non-existent businesses. Cuba is ready for innovative people willing to take chances. The country will attract adventurous entrepreneurs looking for a window of opportunity to establish themselves.

All things considered, the country's infrastructure is good despite current economic problems. Cuba has more than 10 international ports with full service and shipping operating. Thee are adequate highway and and rail systems in place and a telecommunications network which is antiquated but being improved.

Cuba has a large highly-educated labor force. Hired help is affordable. There is a double-tiered economy with Cubans who work in tourism earning dollars. This has created much inequity. Current monthly salaries are low, so there thousands of people yearning to earn decent wages if given the chance. You have to pay a social security tax of about 35% for each worker you hire. Self employment is now legal in many sectors of the economy.

The hottest market which has the potential to produce billions of dollars annually is tourism. The number of tourists visiting Cuba is growing at 30% annually. In the 1950s during the Batista era, Cuba was the most popular tourist destination in the Caribbean. Now, Castro believes that tourism is the salvation for Cuba's economic woes. Cubancan is the organization behind the country's new emphasis on tourism. They have already set the building blocks for a new infrastructure — with improved roads and transportation, a new cruise ship terminal in Havana, new marinas, golf courses, airport expansion and joint foreign investment. There has also been a joint venture hotel boom with foreign corporations contributing to the new infrastructure. About 3 to 5 thousand hotel rooms are being built each year. There is a new emphasis to develop multi-destinations within the island. The government has even offered non-socialistic incentives allowing foreign investors to operate in the country for at least 10 years without paying income tax. Jobs at tourist resorts are highly sought because of the availability of dollars and foreign goods.

Despite the U.S. embargo, Cuba annually has averaged between 1,000,000 and 2,000,000 tourists in recent years. In the last five years tourism has increased 20% annually and become the biggest foreign exchange earner. Currently about two millon tourists generate more than a billion dollars a year. Tourist visits to Cuba have mushroomed from less than 350,000 in 1990 to more than 2 million in 2000. Canada provided the most visitors—170,000 — followed by Italy, Germany Spain and France. This is not to mention all of the Americans who entered through third countries. Tourism has the potential to produce even more money annually as Europeans and Canadians will be joined by more visitors from the U.S. in the future. Cuba now boasts over 30,000 hotel rooms, second only to the Dominican Republic, thanks to a recent tourism building boom. Recent information suggests there will be a shortage of high-quality hotel rooms if tourism continues to grow at its current pace. When the embargo softens tourism will really soar upward. About 150,000 Cubans work in tourism-related businesses.

You should seriously think about investing in this tourism boom. The businesses that are derived from it — bars, restaurants, tours, hotels and outdoor activities are fields worth exploring for investment opportunities. The needs of a burgeoning expatriate community will also give rise to new enterprises. If you have a skill in a particular area perhaps you will be able to put it to use in the 'new' Cuba. If you are experienced in the field of business you choose, you chances for success will greatly increase.

However, you should remember that running a business in a foreign country is lot like managing a one in the U.S. or Canada. Rules, regulations, work ethic, the customs of the people and the way of conducting business will be different than what you expect. You are best advised to try to play by the rules and adapt to the way things work in Cuba. Speaking Spanish will help you immensely when engaging in business transactions and communicating with your help.

Check out restrictions and the tax situation. And most importantly choose a business in which you have a vast prior experience. It's much more difficult to familiarize yourself with a new type of business in a foreign country..

Remember you will be doomed to failure if you try to be an absentee owner. A trustworthy partner or manager can mean the difference in success and failure. Make sure you choose a partner with local experience. Don't trust anyone until you know them and have seen them perform in the workplace. Before forming a partnership you should decide what parts of the business each partner will run in order to avoid problems down the line. Bureaucracy can also be stifling in any foreign country. If you start a business with employees, be aware of your duties and responsibilities as an employer. Know what benefits you will have to pay in addition to salary to avoid problems. The more employees you have, the more headaches you will have.

Before you put a penny of your money into any type of overseas investment there are a few simple rules you should follow. Adhering to these principals will help you make more prudent decisions and protect your investments. Remember as attractive as a foreign investment may seem on the surface, there is always a downside. Bear in mind the rules of doing business vary from country to country. The most important thing you can do is your "homework," that is to say, study the feasibility of your potential investment thoroughly before exchanging any money. Be especially wary of "blue ribbon deals" that appear to be too good to be true. Trust your intuition and gut feeling at times. However, the best strategy and rule of thumb is, "Test before you invest."

Many people will have impossible dreams about what business will be like in Cuba. It is is a giant mistake to assume that success will come easy in Cuba. Also many unforeseen problems will surely arise.

There will be a market for almost any consumer product you can think of. A lot of money will be made in the local market supplying products. Cuba's 11 million people provide a large untapped consumer market. Furthermore, there will soon be a large number of people who are used to U.S. goods and services due to an increasing number of foreign residents and eventual influx of Cuban exiles. All you have to do is find a need and fill it.

## Start-up Business Ideas

Cuba is the most important potential market in the Caribbean. You should take advantage of the opportunities which await you. Start-up costs for a business should be far less than what they are in the US or Canada. Here is a lists of businesses you

may wish to explore. This list should stir your creative juices.
Even if you can't find a business idea to your liking, you may
come up with an even better idea.

Spanish/English language schools
An English, French, German or Italian newspaper
A private bilingual elementary or high school
Business consulting firm
New agricultural products
Internet consulting and web page design
Translating service
Bread and breakfast hotel
Restaurants
Automobile parts
State of the art gas stations
Fast food franchises
Copy centers
Importing used cars from the U.S.
Computer sales and software
Laundry (self-service)
Bicycle shop
Bakery
Money transfers
Housing renovation
Hardware store
Food imports
Toy store
Athletic footware
Private postal service
Secretarial and Typing service
Janitorial and maid service
English bookstore

Charter fishing and scuba diving
Foreign residents association
Travel agency
Super and mini markets
24-hour pharmacy with home delivery
Pizzeria
Celular phones and beepers
Office products and supplies
Offshore bank
Money changing
Furniture factory
Cigar exporting
Swimming pool construction
Real estate office and find-a-home
Satellite T.V. and cable
An English radio station
A driving school
Pawn shop
Voicemail
Desktop publishing
Medical supplies
Mini storage units
New and used furniture rental
Mini storage units
Manufacturing of clothing
Car wash
US and European newspaper distribution
Gringo sports bar
US beauty supplies and cosmetics
Used US clothing
US style department stores
Large newspaper stands

# (ommon Business LING-0

pagos.. . . . . . . . . . . . . . . . . . . . . . . . . . . .Payments, buy on time
Abogado, Licenciado. . . . . . . . . . . . . . . . . . . . . . . . . . . . . . .Lawyer
Acciones. . . . . . . . . . . . . . . . . . . . . . . . . . . . . . . . . . . . . . . . .Stocks
Accionista. . . . . . . . . . . . . . . . . .Stockholder, Shareholder
Activo. . . . . . . . . . . . . . . . . . . . . . . . . . . . . . . . . . . . . . . . . . . .Asset
Agrimensor. . . . . . . . . . . . . . . . . . . . . . . . . . . . . . . .Surveyor
Al contado. . . . . . . . . . . . . . . . . . . . . . . . . . . . . . . . . .For cash
Anualidad. . . . . . . . . . . . . . . . . . . . . . . . . . . . . . . . . . . . .Annuity
Año Fiscal. . . . . . . . . . . . . . . . . . . . . . . . . . . . . . . .Fiscal year
Anticipo, prima, depósito. . . . . . . . . . . . . . . . .Down payment
Arrendamiento. . . . . . . . . . . . . . . . . . . . . . . . . . . . . . . . .Lease
Autenticar. . . . . . . . . . . . . . . . . . . . . . . . . . . . . . . . . . .Notarize
Avalúo. . . . . . . . . . . . . . . . . . . . . . . . . . . . . . . . . . . . .Appraisal
Certificado de depósito. . . . . . . . . . . . . . . . . . . . . . . .C.D.s.
Cheque . . . . . . . . . . . . . . . . . . . . . . . . . . . . . . . . . . .Check
Cláusula . . . . . . . . . . . . . . . . . . . . . . . . . . . . . . . . . . .Clause
Comprador . . . . . . . . . . . . . . . . . . . . . . . . . . . . . . . . . .Buyer
Contrato . . . . . . . . . . . . . . . . . . . . . . . . . . . . . . . . . .Contract
Corredor . . . . . . . . . . . . . . . . .Stockbroker, real estate broker
Costa . . . . . . . . . . . . . . . . . . . . . . . . . . . . . . . . . . . . . . .Cost
Cuenta . . . . . . . . . . . . . . . . . . . . . . . . . . . . . .Bank account
Cuenta Corriente . . . . . . . . . . . . . . . . . . . . .Checking account
Déficit . . . . . . . . . . . . . . . . . . . . . . . . . . . . . .In the red, deficit
Depreciación . . . . . . . . . . . . . . . . . . . . . . . . . . .Depreciation
Deuda . . . . . . . . . . . . . . . . . . . . . . . . . . . . . . . . . . . . .Debt
Divisas . . . . . . . . . . . . . . .Foreign exchange (hard currency)
El Justo Valor del Mercado . . . . . . . . . . . . . . .Fair market value
Embargar, Engancha . . . . . . . . . . . . . . . . . . . . . .Attach assets
En efectivo . . . . . . . . . . . . . . . . . . . . . . . . . . . . . .Pay in cash
Escritura . . . . . . . . . . . . . . . . . . . . . . . . . . . . . . . . . . .Deed
Estado de Cuenta. . . . . . . . . . . . . . .Bank statement, statement
Facilidades de Pago . . . . . . . . . . . . . . . . . . . . .Payment plan
Fideicomiso . . . . . . . . . . . . . . . . . . . . . . . . . . . . . . . .Trust
Fidecomisario . . . . . . . . . . . . . . . . . . . . . . . . . . . . . .Trustee

| | |
|---|---|
| *Financiamiento* | ...Financing |
| *Gastos* | ...Costs, expenses |
| *Giro* | ...Money order |
| *Hipoteca* | ...Mortgage |
| *Impuestos* | ...Taxes |
| *Intereses* | ...Interest |
| *Impuestos Prediales* | ...Property taxes |
| *Inversiones* | ....Investments |
| *Lote.* | ..Lot |
| *Montar, Poner Un Negocio* | ...Start a business |
| *Negocios* | ...Business |
| *Notario* | ...Notary |
| *Pagaré.* | Promissory note |
| *Parcela..* | .Parcel of land |
| *Plazo* | ...Term, period of time |
| *Precio* | ...Price |
| *Préstamo* | ...Loan |
| *Principal.* | ..Principal |
| *Propiedad* | ...Property |
| *Registro..* | .Record of ownership |
| *Renta* | ...Income |
| *Rentabilidad* | ...Profitability |
| *Saldo* | ...Balance of an account |
| *Seguros* | ...Insurance |
| *Socio* | ...Partner |
| *Sociedad* | ....Corporation |
| *Subcontratar* | ..To subcontract, farm out |
| *Superávit* | ...In the black, surplus of capital |
| *Tasa de interés* | ....Interest |
| *Testaferro* | ...Person who lends a name to a business |
| *Terreno* | ...Land |
| *Traspaso* | ...Transfer |
| *Timbres Fiscales* | ....Tax stamps |
| *Valor..* | .Value |
| *Vendedor..* | .Seller |

Before going into business in any foreign country it is a good idea to ask the following questions: Can foreigners own property? What is the cost of labor? What are the country's tax rates? Can foreigners open a bank account? What taxes have to be paid? Does the country provide incentives for investors? Are bank accounts available in US dollars? How reliable is the mail service? Does are skilled employees available? What government agencies help foreign businessmen? Do most businesses have Internet access? Can foreigners own businesses and what are the requirements? Is residency needed to open a business?

Keep in mind that running a business in latin America or any foreign country is not like managing a business in the United States or Canada because of unusual labor laws, the work ethic of the people and the local way of doing business.

If you do decide to start a business, spend a few months analyzing its potential. Don't assume that what works in the U.S. will work abroad. it is important to select a business in which you have a vast prior experience. It's much more difficult to familiarize yourself with a new type of business in a foreign country.

Remember a trustworthy partner or manager can mean the difference in success and failure. So, make sure you choose a partner with local experience. Don't trust anyone until you know them and have seen them perform in the workplace. You will be doomed to failure if you intend to be an absentee owner.

You should learn the local rules of the game. Talk to other people who have been successful in business and learn from them. Profit from their mistakes, experiences and wisdom. Don't rush into anything that seems too good to be true. The best strategy and rule of thumb is to "test before you invest."

There a few indispensable books on the market for anyone thinking of doing business in Latin America. All of these books provide a great deal of business vocabulary and useful phrases that should make doing business easier south of the border. Barron's Talking Business Spanish and the new version Spanish for the Business Traveler are both excellent. Passport Book's Just Enough Business Spanish is also worthwhile. Although English is the second language in Cuba and most of Latin America, you shouldn't assume that everyone speaks it.

In addition, there are other publications which talk about doing business in Latin America. **Latin Trade magazine** is an excellent source for business information. There is an edition in English and one in Spanish. To subscribe write: Latin Trade, First Union Financial Center, 200 South Biscayne Blvd., Suite 1150, Miami, Fl 33131 Tel: (305) 358-8373. Go to any public library or chain bookstore and look for other publications in the business section. Also talk to others who have done business in Cuba to find out what obstacles you may encounter along the way.

## Real Estate

Regulations issued in 1996 legalize private land ownership making it possible to invest in real estate and own property. Consequently most foreigners invest in foreign real estate. Property rights are now recognized and protected from state expropriation. This opens the door for real estate investment and development. There is a potential windfall in redevelopment in Havana or where housing has become substandard. Dilapidated buildings abound, needing new plumbing, water, electrical work and structural redesign.

One area that promises to be a potential gold mine is the run-down decaying buildings which border Havana's sea-side malecón. This area has the potential to become another tourist mecca like Miami's South Beach. It is only a matter of time until this type of transformation will take place.

About 80% of Cubans own their own homes. Those who owned homes before the revolution and stayed have been allowed to keep their homes. Others have acquired homes since then. By law Cubans can trade homes but cannot sell them. The Urban Reform Law of 1960 changed rent payments into mortgage payments on a five to 20 year basis. This made owners out of renters. Today a large percentage of Cubans own their own homes and pay no property taxes.

There is a tremendous housing shortage at present in Havana with some houses and apartments housing several families When looking to invest in land or housing don't assume that the person who is selling land is honest. Proceed with caution. Hire a trustworthy attorney to explain the finer points of local laws. Have your attorney check out any documents and to help you at every stage of negotiations. Make sure he finds out who is the rightful owner of the property and if there are any liens and encumbrances. It is not unusual for scam artists to sell the same piece of property two or three times to different individuals.

Also, be sure to talk to your future neighbors. Ask them about water shortages, safety, burglaries or other problems in the area. Inspect the property in person—never sight un seen. Check to see if you need special permits to build. Be sure to compare land values in your area to see if you are paying a fair price. Make sure that roads and streets are in decent shape and that telephone and electrical services are available if you are building in a remote area. If you can you are wise to rent in your favorite area first in order to find out if it is really for you.

Beach property is always a good investment if you can find it for sale in Cuba. Be sure to check out restrictions when buying property adjacent to the beach. Before you decide to move to an isolated beach area or resort, be aware that the novelty of living at the beach full-time wears off quickly. Visiting the beach for a few days or weeks is very different than living there. The humidity, boredom, lack of emergency medical facilities in isolated areas, tourists and crowds are factors to consider.

The sale of real estate in Cuba is a relatively new addition to the local economy and one that has materialized through the intense demand from visiting tourists.

Recently it was announced for that, for the first time, foreign tourists will be able to buy condominiums and time-share units as a part of a $250 million Canadian-Cuban joint venture. The project, backed by the Cuban government, calls for construction of 2,000 luxury units over the next ten years and is one of the biggest outside investments yet in Cuba's tourism industry.

There will be many new projects with apartments ranging from a simple studio unit to luxurious penthouses, villas and condominiums. All will have swimming pools, garages, central air conditioning, power generators and all of the other amenities of home. Most of the projects currently underway are in the Havana area extending from the eastern beach region to the upscale Miramar area. There are currently no mortgage services available on the island although these services are bound to be available in the not-too-distant future as demand for new housing grows.

At least in the short term, American citizens won't be among those buying into the new resorts. But other foreigners have no such constraints. However, all of this is sure to change once Cuba and the US normalize relations, hopefully in the not too distant future.

Another encouraging sign in the Cuban real estate market is that **REMAX**, which operates one of the biggest chains of world-wide real estate offices, now has an office in Cuba. Their office is found at 7ma esq. 14, Miramar, Tel; (24) 5005, Fax: (24) 5006, E-mail: information@realestate.cuba, website: www.realestatecuba.com. Inmobilaria Aurea in Habana Vieja also has property. You may contact them at: Tel: (53-7) 66-9587, Fax: (53-7) 66-9583. Finally, There is **Real Inmobilaria**, in Miramar at Calle 3 #3407 esq. 36, Tel: (24) 9871, Fax: (24) 9875, E-mail: realin@columbus.cu.

**Coldwell Banker** is also working on eventually establishing offices on the Island. Most certainly the Latin American division of Century 21 will try to set up shop in Cuba. They already have dozens of offices in Mexico and Central America. All of these firms now offer world-wide multiple listing services.

A wealth of information about Cuba's current real estate scene may be found through **Real Estate Cuba**: **www.realestaecuba.com, E-mail:sales@realestatecuba.com**. They offer information about properties for sale, home searches, legal obligations and the real estate business in Cuba. Also see **www.cubaninvestments.com** for real estate opportunities.

The following consortia provide services to ensure every aspect of your real estate purchase is handled professionally, quickly and confidentially:

**HMR & Associates, Ltd.**
P.O. Box 3820
Road Town Tortola
British Virgin Islands
Tel: (284) 494-2544
Fax: (284) 494-2552

**Tour and Marketing International**
Havana Office
Centro de Negocios Zona Franca Mariel
Calle Desamparados No. 166
e/ Habana y Compostela
Oficina No. 320
Cuidad de Habana, Cuba
E-mail:help@primerasinversiones.com

Note: There are some Cubans selling property illegally to foreigners under the table. At this time we don't recommend purchasing property this way since the property remains in the Cuban owner's name and you have no legal recourse if the deal eventually goes sour.

# Havana is Polishing its Old City

HAVANA - The colonial neighborhoods of Old Havana - ground down by years of neglect, lack of money, and salt-laden ocean air - are gradually being restored to the stately buildings that once defined this city as a gateway to the New World. The boom is turning these once crime-ridden, cobblestoned streets into one of the most desirable areas in the country for tourists and Habaneros alike.

To be sure, many of the early benefits are for tourists: new hotels, refurbished parks, and glittering, music-filled restaurants.

But in Castro's Cuba, no rebuilding program, no matter how many foreign tourists and dollars it attracts, can happen without serving a social agenda. In Old Havana, that means moving many of the area's 70,000 residents out of cramped, makeshift dwellings to new housing and teaching them how to live in them, whether they like it or not.

Two blocks from Plaza Vieja, one of the newly restored squares that dot the 525-acre old city, a row of neat townhouses has been built where some displaced families have been sent to live while their buildings are refurbished.

But the residents are also being taught lessons in adjusting to new amenities, such as private bathrooms, a bedroom, or a kitchen with a real stove, sink, and refrigerator. Those are amenities almost unknown in the dense quarters where as many as four families shared one toilet, electricity arrived through a spliced cable, and the sink was a plastic tub.

"These families have become so accustomed to living in close areas and making their own accommodations that they have to understand that their new homes will be different," said Rafael Rojas, director of Old Havana's Master Plan, part of the Municipal Historian's Office, which oversees reconstruction.

"So this is not just about new hotels for travelers, but about creating a whole new living environment for residents," Rojas said.

But other families have had to leave the old neighborhood altogether. When planners conducted a neighborhood census to determine who would be given provisional housing, they discovered thousands of new arrivals, mostly desperate migrants from the provinces who had come seeking better opportunities during Cuba's economic crisis in the mid-1990s.

Families originally from Old Havana - and they must prove it with government documentation - are given first priority to stay in a renovated building. Thousands of others have been reassigned to new housing developments in Alamar, an eastern suburb about 10 miles outside Havana, or they have been sent back to their provinces.

The payoff for Cuba's growing tourist industry has been dramatic. Old Havana, nestled along the capital's sea-splashed boulevard, has become the country's second most important tourist magnet, outdone only by Varadero, the resort city about 80 miles east, a favorite winter sanctuary for planeloads of Europeans and Canadians.

Old Havana's narrow cobblestone streets, colonial churches, forts, and elegant houses are reminiscent of Beacon Hill, Quebec City, or Cartagena in Colombia. But preserving the neighborhood's charm was rarely a priority for corrupt governments in the 1930s and '40s and hard to justify for Fidel Castro's communist regime, which promised more housing when it seized power in 1959. It allowed multiple families to inhabit dwellings that were once large single-family homes.

Despite Old Havana's crumbling condition, the United Nations placed it on its World Heritage List of special places in 1982 and gave the government money to begin restoration. But it took another decade for the Historian's Office to get the funds and permission it needed from Castro to turn the area into an attractive opportunity for foreign investors.

Only a third of Old Havana has been touched by the magic wand of Habaguanex. There is much in the old neighborhood, as in most of this city of 2 million people, that is crumbling. And some residents in other sections of the city wonder when or if they will get the kind of attention that the zona turistica has seen.

"I used to feel lucky that I didn't live in Old Havana, because it wasn't very nice or safe," said Yeslinda Lara, 30, a government secretary from the Vedado neighborhood. "But now I see all of the scaffolding and the new buildings, and it makes me wish I lived there. Or at least that someone would come do that where I live."

* *Courtesy of Central America Weekly*

# New Investment Laws

In 1993 Cuba opened up a large international market by legalizing the U.S. dollar. The dollar now accounts for about two-thirds of the Cuban economy. This dollar currency is mainly geared towards tourism and resident foreigners and Cubans holding dollars. Remittances by Cubans abroad to relatives in Cuba account for about $400 million annually.

Originally a statute was passed in 1982 authorizing foreign investments in Cuba in the form of joint ventures with a state enterprise. Next, the constitution was amended in 1992 and laws passed to provide guarantees for foreign investors including repatriation of profits to remove the state's monopoly on foreign trade and to modify labor legislation, particularly for tourism.

**Cubanacán** (*Corporación de Turismo y Comercio Internacional*) is in charge of linking foreign companies wishing to invest in joint ventures in the Cuban tourist sector. Joint ventures in Cuba work like this: any Cuban entity retains 51% of the control when a foreign company invests in the country. In some instances the percentage of foreign ownership was approved at a level above 50%. However, at that time foreigners could not hold the majority interest in a joint venture(joint ventures with private individuals in Cuba are illegal). These joint ventures were part of the process of steady economic reform to move Cuba in the direction of market capitalism. By the end of 1995 there were over two hundred joint ventures operating in Cuba. Canada, Spain, Italy and Mexico are the most active countries in the joint venture program. Most of these ventures have been in the area of tourism. However, there has also been substantial investment in mining and agricultural operations.

Cuba has further tried to woo investors in recent years by offering incentives. In September of 1995 the Cuban National Assembly passed a new investment law (Law Number 77) giving foreign investors the right to operate wholly owned enterprises in most sectors of the economy. This law confirmed the Cuban government's commitment to encourage and facilitate foreign investments. According to this law foreigners were permitted to operate a business without creating a joint venture. Currently there are 350 joint ventures worth $2.6 billion operating in the country. The majority are with companies from Spain, Canada, Italy, the United Kingdom and Mexico

Under this law investments may be made in real estate which may be used for residential or office purposes for foreigners. Investments can also be made in real property to be used in tourism operations. However, under the new agreement, buildings may be purchased, but not land.

The only areas where foreign investment was not permitted were education, health and the military.

This new law was the first step in moving the country toward a real market economy. It is part of an ongoing process of economic reform in Cuba. It replaced the 1982 statute which created joint ventures and is much broader and more flexible in its scope. The new law virtually increased the role of foreign investment in the economy creating free trade zones in Havana in 1996 and allowing foreign companies to invest in parts of the economy previously off limits. Now individual investors or companies may create an affiliate or subsidiary of a foreign firm. This law virtually opens all sectors of the Cuban economy to foreign investment with a few exceptions. The three exceptions are: health services, public education and the armed forces.

Law 77 provides guarantees and security for the investor by prohibiting expropriation of foreign investments except when such action is for a public use or in public interest, which may be declared by the government in accordance with provisions of the constitution, legislation and international agreements. Furthermore, before expropriation may take place, the investor must be compensated for the commercial value of the property which is to be established by mutual accord. This measure should ease the fears of those foreign investors who are afraid to invest in the country because of the possibility of government expropriation. They can now feel more secure about investing in Cuba.

There are specific taxes and fees of around 30% of net earnings, and an employment and social security tax. These taxes and fees must be paid by foreign owned and joint enterprises. There are also incentives for reinvestment provided by this law.

We have conveniently listed the complete version of Law 77 at the end of this chapter to help clarify any questions the reader may have.

Foreign investors who wish to establish a wholly owned enterprise must initially apply through the **Ministry of Foreign Investment and Economic Cooperation** (MINVEC).

This agency is responsible for governing and controlling the foreign investment process, the development of free zones and industrial parks, the promotion of all foreign investment, and guiding the negotiating process when setting up foreign investment.

Government authorization is necessary and there are a series of steps and layers of government involved. Both wholly owned enterprises and joint ventures have to be approved by MINVEC. Then they have to be evaluated by the Council of Ministers. The whole process can take up to a year to get approval and set up a joint venture in Cuba.

Spanish, French, Canadians and others have invested extensively in tourism despite the embargo. They have realized that Cuba is a prime Caribbean market and began to carve up Cuba for themselves during the first half of the 90's by investing in tourism and other areas. American companies anxious to get a toe hold in Cuba are already lining up.

Here is a list of organizations which provide information about doing business in Cuba:

**U.S. - Cuba Trade and Economic Council**, Inc., 30 Rockefeller Plaza, New York, NY 10112-0002, Tel: (212) 246-1444, Fax: 9212) 246-2345, e-mail usctec@aol.com. It is the only organization in the U.S. to help individuals seeking advice about doing business in Cuba. They will furnish technical support, a wealth of information and assistance.

They have several publications available through their web page at : www. cuba trade.org. We recommend checking out this site and all that it has to offer. Cuba Foreign Trade is published quarterly by the Chamber of Commerce of Cuba. The focus of the magazine is on foreign trade and general issues of commercial interest. It lists many business contacts and potential business opportunities in different fields. Business Tips on Cuba is another of their publications which potential investors should read. Economic Eye On Cuba is published each Monday for the members of the U.S.-Cuba Trade and Economic Council.

The **Cámara de Comercio de la República de Cuba** or Cuban Chamber of Commerce publishes a yearly directory of companies who trade within Cuba, a list of contacts, addresses and telephone numbers of each importer. Cuban Chamber of Commerce, Calle 21 esq. A #661, Vedado, La Habana, Cuba, Tel: (537) 55-1321, Fax: (537) 33-3042, www.camaracuba.cubaweb.cu,

Another excellent source of information is **Berkshire Financial Services, Inc.**, Apdo. 1500 World Trade Center, Panama City, Panama, Tel: (507) 317-0037, Fax: (507) 317-0036, E-mail: info@berkshire-financial.com, www.berkshire-financial.com. They also publish an excellent book called Cuban capitalism - A Guide to Trade and Investment in Pre and Post Embargo Cuba.

**Consultores Asociados S.A.**, 5th Ave. Esquina 164 # 16210 Playa Miramar, Havana, Cuba tel: 33-6011, Fax: 33-6012

**Oficina Nacional TIPS/Cuba**, calle 30, # 302, Esquina a 3ra. Miramar, Havana, Cuba Tel; 33-1797, Fax: 33-1799.

**CARIB IMPEX** imports and exports both Cuban products and services. They can help you find distributors for products in Cuba and to establish solid commercial ties with Cuban firms. They are based in the Bahamas at CARIB IMPEX, Northfolk House,third floor, Frederick Street, P.O. Box N-9455, Bahamas, Tel: (2420 356-7270) Fax; (242) 356-2587, E-mail:carib@batelnet.bs.

There is a very helpful website at: www.cubaweb.com which acts as a clearing house for those who want to find out about doing business in Cuba. Check out this great website for a wealth of information. You may e-mail them at rosamaria@cubaweb.com.

You should also see www.cubaadvice.com. They offer help for businessmen in Cuba and have an office center with fax and e-mail which you may use.

Cuba's monthly business magazine, Business Tips on Cuba, is full of information about investment opportunities in Cuba. It is published in several languages including English. See www.tips.cu.

# How Find a Lawyer in Latin America

Cuba's legal system is based on American and Spanish law mixed with communist legal theory. If you plan to go into business or buy or sell property in Cuba you will most certainly need the services of an attorney. Your lawyer will be able to help you understand the complexities of Cuba's legal system. An attorney is one of the best investments you can make because he or she can assist you with bureaucratic procedures and handle other legal matters that may arise. If you are not fully bilingual, be sure to choose a lawyer who is.

It is very important to watch your lawyer closely, since lawyers in Latin America tend to drag their feet as other bureaucrats do. Never take anything for granted. Refuse to believe that things are getting done, even if you are assured they are. Check with your lawyer on a regular basis and ask to see your file to make sure he has taken care of your business. As you might imagine paper work moves slowly in Cuba. You don't want a procrastinating lawyer to prolong the process.

When you first contact a lawyer, make sure he is accessible at all hours. Also be sure you have your lawyer's office and home telephone number in case you need him in an emergency. If your lawyer is always in meetings or out of the office, this is a clear sign your work is being neglected and you have chosen the wrong attorney.

Take your time and look around for an attorney. Ask friends, foreigners and other knowledgeable people for the names of their lawyers. Then try to inquire about your potential lawyer's reputation and integrity.

All over the world there are always a few incompetent, unscrupulous attorneys, so be careful who you are dealing with before you make your final choice. One of the most important people in your life in Cuba will be your lawyer, so it is important to develop a good working relationship.

The restrictions preventing foreign lawyers from practicing in Cuba has been somewhat relaxed. We have heard that some foreign lawyers are practicing in free-trade zones.

In any event, if you plan to invest or do business in Cuba, you should purchase Diccionario de Términos Legales (Dictionary of Legal Terms), to help you understand legal language.

In Cuba **Consultoría Jurídica Internacional** (International Judicial Consultative Bureau) Calle 18 #120, corner of Ave. 3, Miramar, Havana, Tel; 33-2490, Fax: 33-2303 and Ave 1 #208, in

Varadero tel; 33-7077 Fax: 33-7080 offers legal advice for all aspects of Cuban law including marriages, contracts and joint business ventures. The will also represent you. They have offices in Havana, Pinar del Río, Varadero, Villa Clara, Cienfuegos Camgüey, Ciego de Avila, Holguín, Bayamo and Santiago de Cuba.

If you are seeking a United States based attorney to help you with legal question about going into business in Cuba we suggest you contact **McConnel Valdés** — the world's largest Hispanic-owned law firm. They can assist clients in understanding the present legal restrictions affecting individuals and companies doing business in Cuba. They can also prepare clients for the day when such restrictions are lifted. Mr. Ramón Coto-Ojeda is the person to contact at this law firm. McConnel Valdéz, P.O. Box 364225, San Juan, Puerto Rica 00936-4225, Tel: (787) 759-9292, Fax: (787) 759-9225, E-mail: iln@mcypr.com, Internet: http://www.mcypr.com.

The following U.S. based attorneys also have expertise in the field of Cuba:

**Mr. Adolpho R. García**
Partner Mcdermott, Will & Emery
28 State Street, 33rd Floor
Boston, MA 02109
tel: (617) 353-4070
Fax; (617) 535-3800
E-mail: agarcia@mwe.com

**Mr. David Baron**
Senior Associate
McDermott, Will & Emery
600 13th Street N. W.
Washington, D.C. 20005-3096
Tel: (202) 756-8102
Fax: (202) 756-8087
E-mail: dbaron@mwe.com

**Mr. Robert L. Muse, Esq.**
Law Offices of Robert L. Muse
Suite M-2
1320 19th Street, Northwest
Washington, D.C. 20036
Tel: (202) 887-4990
Fax: (202) 861-6912

# LAW NUMBER 77
# FOREIGN INVESTMENT ACT

INDEX

# CHAPTER I
## PURPOSE AND CONTENT

**Article 1.1** This act has the purpose of promoting and encouraging foreign investment in the territory of the Republic of Cuba, in order to carry out profitable activities which contribute to the country's economic capacity and sustainable development, on the basis of respect for the country's sovereignty and independence, and the protection and rational use of natural resources; and of establishing, for that purpose, the basic legal regulation under which this can be realized.

**2.** The norms contained in this act comprise, among other elements, the guarantees granted to investors, the sectors of the economy which can receive foreign investments, the forms in which they can be utilized, the various types of investments relating to banking, taxation and labor and the norms related to the protection of the environment and the rational use of natural resources.

# CHAPTER II
## GLOSSARY

**Article 2.** This act recognizes the following terms and their definitions:

a) International economic association:
Joint action by one or more national investors and one or more foreign investors within the national territory for the production of goods, the offering of services or both for profit, in its two forms, which consist of joint ventures and international economic association contracts.

b) Authorization:
Documentation issued by the Executive Committee of the Council of Ministers or a Government Commission for the realization of

one of the forms of foreign investment authorized by this act for a specific period.

c) Foreign capital:
Capital originating outside the country, as well as part of the profits or dividends belonging to the foreign investor which are reinvested in accordance with this act.

d) Top management posts:
Positions belonging to members of the management and administration of the joint ventures totally foreign capital company as well as the representatives of the parties to international economic association contracts and the management personnel of totally foreign capital companies.

e) Government Commissions:
Commissions designated by the Executive Committee of the Council of Ministers with the authority to approve foreign capital investments in its area of competence, as stipulated in this act.

f) Administrative concessions:
Unilateral action on the part of the Government of the Republic, whereby an entity is granted the right to exploit a public service or a natural resource, or to build or utilize a public work under the terms and conditions to be determined.

g) International economic association contract:
Pact or agreement among one or more national investors and one or more foreign investors, for the realization of actions fitting an international economic association, even without the establishment of a legal entity distinct from each of the parties.

h) Totally foreign capital company:
Commercial entity with foreign capital, without the involvement of any national investor.

i) Joint venture:
Cuban commercial company which adopts the form of a nominal share corporation, in which one or more national investors and one or more foreign investors participate.

j) Employing entity:
Cuban organization with legal status, authorized to establish a contract with a joint venture or a totally foreign company, through which it supplies, at the company's request, the workers of various skills needed by the company, who are employed by that organization.

k) Assets:
Wages, income and other remuneration, as well as increases, compensations and other additional payments received by Cuban and foreign workers, with the exception of those stemming from the economic stimulation fund, if it exists.

l) Foreign investment:
Capital imput by foreign investors, in any of the forms stipulated by this act.

m) Foreign investor:
The person or corporation, with a foreign domicile and foreign capital, which becomes a shareholder in a joint venture or participates in a totally foreign capital company, or which is party to an international economic association contract.

n) National investor:
State company or entity with legal status, a corporaton of other Cuban national entity whose address is in national territory and which becomes a shareholder of a joint venture or is party to an international economic association contract.

## CHAPTER III
## GUARANTEES FOR INVESTORS

**Article 3:** The foreign investor within Cuban national territory enjoys full protection and security, and their assets cannot be expropriated except for reasons of the public good or in the interest of society, as declared by the government, in accordance with the Constitution of the Republic, current legislation, an international agreement covering the actual promotion and protection of investments undertaken in Cuba. In the case of expropriation, indemnification is made in freely convertible currency and is equal to the commercial value established by mutual agreement.

If an agreement is not reached, the price is set by an organization with internationally recognized prestige in the assessment of business assets, authorized by the Ministry of Finance and Prices and contracted for that purpose with the assets of all parties or of the foreign investor and the Ministry of Foreign Investment and Economic Cooperation, if the affected party is a totally foreign capital company.

**Article 4.1** The period of time granted for the development of operations by a joint venture, the parties to an international economic association contract or a totally foreign capital company, can be extended by the same authority that authorizes the entities, as long as it is requested by the interested parties before the end of the period.

**2.** If the period is not extended at the time of its expiration the joint venture, international economic association contract or foreign capital company shall be liquidated, as stipulated in the constituent documents and existing legislation and the proportion due to the foreign investor shall be paid in freely convertible currency, except in the case of an express agreement to the contrary.

**Article 5.** Foreign investments are equally protected against third party reclamation which comply with the law and are in accordance with Cuban laws and rulings of national courts of justice.

**Article 6.1** At any moment, subject to the consent of all parties, the foreign investor in an international economic association can sell or transfer its total or partial share of the company to the state or a third party, subject to government authorization, receiving the corresponding price in freely convertible currency, except in the case of an express agreement to the contrary.

**2.** The foreign investor in a totally foreign capital company can at any moment sell or transfer, in any form, to the state or a third party and subject to authorization by the government, its total or partial share of the company, receiving the corresponding price in freely convertible currency, except in the case of an express agreement to the contrary.

**Article 7.** The corresponding price to be paid to the foreign investor, in the cases discussed in Articles 4 and 6 of this act, is set with the consent of both parties, or when that is not feasible, by an organization with internationally recognized prestige in the assessment of businesses and authorized by the Ministry of Finance and Prices to operate in national territory, and contracted for that purpose jointly by all parties, or by agreement of the foreign investor in a totally foreign capital company and the Ministry of Foreign Investment and Economic Cooperation.

**Article 8.** The state guarantees the foreign investor the free transfer abroad, in freely convertible currency, free from taxes or any fee related to such transfer of:

(a) net profits or dividends obtained as a result of the investment; and (b) The monies due him or her in the cases discussed in Articles 3, 4, and 6 of this Act.

**2.** foreign citizens working in a joint venture, for the parties in any other form of international economic associations or in a totally foreign capital company, as long as they are not permanent residents in Cuba, have the right to transfer abroad the income they receive, within stipulated amounts and according to the other regulations issued by the Bank of Cuba.

**Article 9.** Joint ventures and the parties to international economic association contracts are obliged to pay taxes in line with the special regulations stipulated by this Act, until the expiration of the period for which they were authorized.

The stipulations made in the previous paragraph are not applicable to the rates, contributions (with the exception of social security contributions) and formal duties established in current legislation, nor to the payment obligations included in the Mining Act of December 21, 1994, or other legal provisions which may be issued in regard to natural resources, which shall be observed in the manner and extent stipulated in those laws.

## CHAPTER IV
## SECTORS OPEN TO FOREIGN INVESTMENT

**Article 10.** Foreign investments may be authorized in all sectors, excluding health and education services for the population and the armed forces institutions, with the exception of the latter's commercial system.

## CHAPTER V
## FOREIGN INVESTMENTS

## FIRST SECTION
## MANIFESTATIONS AND FORMS OF
## FOREIGN INVESTMENT

**Article 11.** For the purposes of this Act, foreign investments are defined as:

a) Direct investments, through which the foreign investor participates in an effective manner in the management of joint venture or totally foreign capital company, and through which the foreign investor makes his or her own contributions in international economic association contracts.

b) Any investments in stocks or other securities or bonds, either public or private, which do not fit the definition of direct investment.

**Article 12.** Foreign investment shall adopt one of the following forms:
a) Joint venture
b) International economic association contract
c) Totally foreign capital company.

## SECOND SECTION
## JOINT VENTURES

**Article 13.1** Joint ventures imply the establishment of a legal status distinct from that of any one of the parties. They adopt the form of nominal share corporations and current legislation in this field applies to them.

**2.** The proportions of capital stock which should be contributed by the foreign investor and the national investor are agreed upon by both partners and defined as part of the authorization.

**3.** The establishment of a joint venture must take the form of a public document, and annexed to this notarized document include the agreement of economic associations, the bylaws governing the company and the authorization.

The agreement of economic association contains the fundamental pacts between the partners for the realization and development of the joint venture's operations, and for the achievement of its objectives, among them the guarantees of Cuban participation or joint administration of the company and the assurances of a market for the company's products or services: the bases of its accounting system and the estimate and distribution of profits.

The joint ventures bylaws shall include provisions related to the corporation's organization and operation, which must cover the general shareholder's meeting, its characteristics and organization: the necessary quorum and the requirements for exercising the right to vote at the general shareholder's meeting: the structure and characteristics of the management and administrative body; the method by which these bodies make their decisions, both in general shareholder's meetings and within the management and administrative body, which could range from a simple majority to unanimity; provisions for dissolution and the procedure for liquidating the company; as well as other stipulations resulting from the current legislation in the field .

4. If the public document does not designate the person or persons who shall administer the joint venture, the first general shareholder's meeting can be held and the members of the management and administrative body can be designated in line with the bylaws.

5. Once the joint venture is created , the partners cannot be changed except with the consent of the parties and the approval of the authority that granted the authorization.
A change of partners is defined as the substitution of the foreign partner by another person or company, or of the Cuban partner by another person or company.

6. Joint ventures can establish offices, representations, branch offices and affiliates, in national territory and abroad, as well as participating in entities abroad.

7. A joint enterprise acquires legal status when it is included in the Registry maintained by the Republic of Cuba's Chamber of Commerce regarding these activities.

## THIRD SECTION
## INTERNATIONAL ECONOMIC
## ASSOCIATION CONTRACTS

**Article 14.1** International economic association contracts have the following characteristics, among others:

a) They do not imply a legal entity separate from those of the contracting parties.

b) They may have the objective of carrying out any activity authorized by the contracting parties.

c) The contracting parties are free to stipulate all the pacts and clauses that they deem to be in accordance with their interests, as long as they do not infringe on the authorized objective, the conditions of the authorization or current legislation.

d) Each contracting party makes separate contributions, which constitute a cumulative amount which they own at all times and even though they do not constitute capital stock, it is in their interest to establish a common fund, as long as the portion of ownership belonging to each of the parties is well defined.

**2.** The text of the contract states the proportion of taxes to be paid by each party and the times of the year in which profits are distributed among them, after meeting the fiscal obligations, as well as the responsibility for losses, if there are any.

**3.** In an international economic association contract, the party which carries out an act of management which benefits all parties is fully responsible to third parties, but among the parties each one is responsible to the extent or proportion stipulated in the contract.

**4.** Once an international economic association contract is granted, the participants cannot be changed, except with the agreement of the parties and the approval of the authority that granted the authorization.

**5.** An international economic association contract must be presented in the form of a public document in order to be approved and goes into effect the moment it is included in the registry maintained by the Republic of Cuba's Chamber of Commerce regarding these activities.

## FOURTH SECTION
## TOTALLY FOREIGN CAPITAL COMPANY

**Article 15.1** In the totally foreign capital company, the foreign investor manages the company, enjoys all the rights pertinent to it and is responsible for all the obligations described in the authorization.

**2.** The foreign investor involved in a totally foreign capital company may act as an individual or a corporation within Cuban national territory:

a) Through the creation of a foreign entity of which the investor is the owner, within the form of a stock corporation and by being included in the Registry of the Republic of Cuba's Chamber of Commerce.

b) By being included in the Republic of Cuba's Chamber of Commerce and acting independently.

## CHAPTER VI
## REAL ESTATE INVESTMENTS

**Article 16.1** Under the authorization of this Act, investments can be made in real estate and acquire ownership and other property rights over that real estate.

**2.** The investment in real estate discussed in the previous paragraph can be utilized for:

a) Housing and other structures destined for private residence or tourism activities of persons who are not permanent residents in Cuba.

b) Housing or offices of foreign companies.

c) Real estate development for use in tourism.

**Article 17.** Investments consisting of the purchase of real estate which constitutes corporate activity are considered direct investments.

**Article 18.** The conditions and terms under which the purchase and transfer of real estate discussed in Article 16 of this Act are determined in the authorization and must be in accord with current legislation.

## CHAPTER VII
## CONTRIBUTIONS AND THEIR VALUE

**Article 19.1** For the purposes of this Act, contributions are defined as the following:

a) Freely convertible currency.

b) Machinery, equipment or other physical or tangible goods.

c) Intellectual property rights and other rights over intangible goods.

d) Property rights over personal items and real estate, and other rights over these, including surface rights.

e) Other goods and rights.

The contributions which do not consist of freely convertible currency shall be assessed in that currency.

**2.** Transfer in favor of national investors of property and other rights over state property, for the purposes of contributions by them, shall be carried out under the principles established in the Constitution of the Republic, and under the prior certification of the Ministry of Finance and Prices, in consultation with the corresponding agency and with the approval of the Executive Committee of the Council of Ministers.

The payments of intellectual property rights and other rights over intangible goods shall be covered by current legislation on this matter.

**3.** Payments in freely convertible currency are set according to their value on the international market and conversion into the national currency, for accounting purposes, shall be realized according to the national bank of Cuba's exchange rates. The freely convertible currency which constitutes payment of foreign capital should enter the country through the authorized banking entity for use in the national territory.

**4.** The payments which are not made in freely convertible currency, except those consisting of intellectual property rights and other rights over intangible goods, and which are destined for the capital stock of joint enterprises, or which constitute payments in international economic association contracts, are valued according to the methods freely agreed upon by investors. Their value can be determined with the aid of the corresponding expert certification drawn up by the entities under the authority of the Ministry of Finance and Prices.

**5.** The evaluation of the contributions that are not made in freely convertible currency, except for those in payment for intellectual property rights and other rights over intangible goods, is always made with the aid of expert certification drawn up by entities under the authority of the Minister of Finance and Prices.

**6.** Payments consisting of intellectual property and other rights over intangible goods shall be assessed by methods fully agreed upon by all the national and international investors and between the foreign investor and the Ministry of Foreign Investment and Economic Cooperation, in the case of payments to a totally foreign capital enterprise.

## CHAPTER VIII
## NEGOTIATIONS AND AUTHORIZATION
## OF FOREIGN INVESTMENT

**Article 20.1.** For the creation of an international economic association, the national investor must negotiate with the foreign investor every aspect of the investment, including its economic feasibility, the respective payments, the associations form of management and administration, as well as the legal document needed for its formalization.

**2.** In the case of a total foreign capital company, the Ministry of Foreign Investment and Economic Cooperation indicates to the investor the responsible Cuban entity in the sector, subsector of economic activity for which the investment is planned, and the investor must analyze its proposition with that entity and obtain the corresponding written approval.

**Article 21.1.** Authorization for foreign investments in national territory is granted by the Executive Committee of the Council of Ministers, or by a commission designated for that purpose.

**2.** The Executive Committee of the Council of Ministers has the exclusive power to authorize foreign investments in any of the sectors listed below or those with the following characteristics:

a) When the total sum of the payments made by foreign and national investors is greater than the equivalent of ten (10) million U.S. dollars in freely convertible currency.

b) In the case of totally foreign capital companies

c) Investments made in public services such as transportation, communication, aqueducts, electricity, or for the construction or exploitation of a public work.

d) When a foreign company with capital shares owned by a foreign state is involved.

e) When the investment involves the exploitation of a natural resource, in accordance with legislation for the protection of the environment and rational use of natural resources.

f) Investments which include the transfer of state property or a real right which is the property of the State.

g) In the case of the armed forces' commercial system.

3. The Government Commission has the power to authorize foreign investments not mentioned in the previous paragraph.

**Article 22.** The foreign investor who expects to obtain authorization for a totally foreign capital company shall present its request, jointly with the corresponding Cuban entity, and to the Minister of Foreign Investment and Economic Cooperation.

**Article 23.1.** To set up a joint venture or to establish an international economic association contract, the written request should be presented jointly to the Ministry of Foreign Investment and Economic Cooperation by the foreign investor and the national investor.

**2.** The investment request is presented along with the following documents.

a) For the establishment of joint ventures and the granting of international economic association contracts: draft versions of economic association agreement and the bylaws of the proposed joint venture or the contract to be granted, as well as an economic feasibility study, in both cases.

b) In regard to the foreign investor: documentation attesting to his or her identity and solvency, as well as proof that he or she is a legitimate representative of corporations, when applicable.

c) In regard to the national investor, in the case of a state enterprise or entity: express written acceptance granted by the maximum authority in the sector, subsector or economic activity in which the foreign investment is being made; in the case of a commercial association or civilian service organization based on totally Cuban capital, express authorization of the general shareholders' meeting which grants specific authority to sign the corresponding documents with the foreign investor.

d) When the foreign investor proposes the constitution of a totally foreign capital company: acceptance by the maximum authority of the sector, subsector or economic activity for which the investment is planned, the text of the bylaws, an economic feasibility study, documentation attesting to the foreign investor's identity and solvency, and in the case of a corporation, proof that the foreign investor is a legitimate representative authorized to make the specific investment.

e) The document accompanying the investment request must be duly authenticated, when pertinent.

**3.** In order for the Ministry of Foreign Investment and Economic Cooperation to accept the request, it must be presented with the formalities described in the present Article.

**4.** Once the request is accepted by the Ministry of Foreign Investment and Economic Cooperation, it shall be submitted for consultation to all the corresponding agencies and institutions in order to obtain their report on matters pertinent to them.

**5.** Once the above procedures are completed, the Ministry of Foreign Investment and Economic Cooperation shall refer the accumulated documentation and its evaluation to the Executive Committee of the Council of Ministers of the Government Commission, as the case may be, so that it may make the pertinent decision.

**6.** The decision denying or approving the foreign investment is handed down within a period of 60 days from the date on which the request was presented, and the applicants are notified.

**Article 24.1.** The authorization contains the conditions under which it is granted and the objective and time period of the form of investment in question.

**2.** If the objective of the approved investment is the exploitation of a public service or a natural resource, or the construction and exploitation of a public work, the Executive Committee of the Council of Ministers may grant the corresponding administrative concession, under the terms and conditions it establishes.

**Article 25.** The conditions established in the authorization can be clarified through the Ministry of Foreign Investment and Economic Cooperation, at the request of the parties.

## CHAPTER IX
## THE BANKING SYSTEM

**Article 26.1.** Joint ventures, foreign investors and national investors which are party to international economic association contracts, jointly or individually, and totally foreign capital companies shall open accounts in freely convertible currency in any bank in the National Banking System, through which they shall receive and make payments related to their operations.

2. Joint ventures and national investors who are parties to international economic association contracts may open accounts in freely convertible currency in banks located abroad, with the authorization of the National Bank of Cuba.

**Article 27.** Joint ventures, parties to international economic association contracts and totally foreign capital companies can be authorized on an exceptional basis by the Executive Committee of the Council of Ministers to effect certain changes and payments in nonconvertible national currency.

**Article 28.** Joint ventures, foreign investors and national investors who are parties to international economic association contracts, and totally foreign capital companies can arrange loans in foreign currency:

a) With a bank in the National Banking System of a financial entity approved by the National Bank of Cuba.

b) With banks or financial entities abroad, in accordance with existing legal regulations covering this matter.

## CHAPTER X
## EXPORT AND IMPORT SYSTEM

**Article 29.** Joint ventures, national and foreign investors who are parties to international economic association contracts, and totally foreign capital companies have the right, in accordance with established legislation in the field, to export their products directly and to import, also directly, whatever is needed for their purpose.

# CHAPTER XI
# LABOR SYSTEM

**Article 30.** Foreign investment activities must observe the labor and social security legislation in effect in Cuba, with the adjustments included in this Act.

**Article 31.1** The workers in activities corresponding to foreign investments shall be, as a rule, Cubans or foreigners permanently residing in Cuba.

**2.** However, the management and administrative bodies of joint ventures or totally foreign capital companies, or the parties to international economic association contracts, may determine that certain top administrative positions or some posts of a technical nature shall be filled by persons who are not permanent residents in the country and in those cases, determine the labor conditions to be applied and the rights and obligations of those workers.

Nonpermanent residents in the country who are contracted are subject to the country's current legislation covering immigration and foreigners.

**Article 32.1.** Joint ventures, the parties to international economic association contracts and totally foreign capital companies may be authorized to create an economic stimulus fund for Cubans or permanent residents in Cuba who are working in activities corresponding to foreign investments.

**2.** The contributions to the economic stimulus fund shall be made out of earned profits. The amount of these contributions shall be agreed upon between the joint ventures, foreign investors and national investors who are party to international economic association contracts and totally foreign capital companies, and the Minister of Foreign Investment and Economic Cooperation.

**Article 33.1** The workers in joint ventures who are Cuban or permanent residents in Cuba, with the exception of the members of management or administrator, are contracted by an employing entity proposed by the Ministry of Foreign Investment and Economic Cooperation, and authorized by the Minister of Labor and Social Security.

The members of management or administration of joint venture are designated by the general shareholders' meeting and hired directly by the joint venture.

Only in the exceptional case, with the proper authorization, may a joint venture directly employ persons who work in that company, and always in accordance with current legal provisions in the field of hiring.

**2.** The persons working for the parties to international economic association contracts are contracted by the Cuban party, in accordance with current legal provisions in the field of employment.

**3.** In totally foreign capital companies, the services of Cuban workers and foreign workers residing permanently in Cuba, with exception of the members of the management and administrative body, shall be hired through a contract between the company and an employing entity proposed by the Minister of Foreign Investment and Economic Cooperation, and authorized by the Ministry of Labor and Social Security.

The members of the management and administration of the totally foreign capital company are designated by the company and hired by it.

**4.** Payments to Cuban workers and foreign workers residing permanently in Cuba are made in national currency which must be obtained beforehand from convertible foreign currency, except in the case described in Article 27 of this Act.

**Article 34.1.** The employing entity discussed in the previous Article individually contracts and directly hires Cuban workers and permanent residents. This employing entity pays those workers their wages.

**2.** When a joint venture or totally foreign capital company considers that a specific worker does not meet the requirements of the job, it can request the employing entity to replace that worker with another. Any labor dispute is settled with the employing entity, which pays the worker, at its own expense, the indemnification to which he or she is entitled, determined by the competent authorities. In pertinent cases, the joint venture or totally foreign capital company compensates the employing entity for such payments, in accordance with the procedure established, and always in compliance with existing legislation.

**Article 35.** Notwithstanding what is stipulated in the preceding articles of this Chapter, the authorization approving the foreign investment can in exceptional cases establish special labor regulations.

**Article 36.** The technological advances consisting of innovations and other tangible goods which are covered by intellectual property law and which are developed within the framework of an international economic association or by Cuban workers in a foreign capital company are covered under current legislation.

**Article 37.** The Ministry of Labor and Social Security is empowered to issue as many complementary legal provisions as it considers necessary for the best application of what is described in this Chapter, especially in the fields of hiring and labor discipline.

# CHAPTER XII
## SPECIAL TAXATION AND DUTIES SYSTEM

**Article 38.** Joint ventures, foreign investors and national investors who are parties to an international economic association contract are subject to the following fiscal obligations:

a) Income tax.
b) Tax covering the utilization of the labor force and contributions to social security.
c) Customs duties and other payments.
d) Land transportation tax, covering the ownership or possession of land motor vehicles.
e) Documents tax, which covers rates and payments when applying for, obtaining or renewing certain documents.

**Article 39.** For the purpose of this Act, the payment of taxes by the persons and companies mentioned in the previous Article carries the following characteristics:

a) Income taxes are levied at a rate of (30%) of net taxable income. In cases considered in the nation's interest, the Executive Committee of the Council of Ministers can exempt all or part of the tax on net income that is reinvested in the country.

b) When the exploitation of renewable or nonrenewable natural resources involved, the income tax rate can be raised by decision of the Executive Committee of the Council of Ministers. In that case, the taxation rate can be raised as high as fifty percent (50%).

c) In regard to the tax on utilization of the labor force and social security contributions, the following is established:

**1.** For utilization of the labor force, a discount is granted in the current taxation rate, to a rate of 11%.

2. Social security contributions are covered by a taxation rate of 14%.

3. The taxation rates expressed in the two previous clauses are applied on the total wages and other income from any source received by the workers, except what is turned over to them as economic stimulus.

d) Foreign investors who are partners in joint ventures or parties to international economic association contracts are exempt from paying taxes on personal income obtained from a business' profit.

**Article 40.** The totally foreign capital company is obliged throughout the duration of its operations to pay taxes in accordance with current tax legislation.

**Article 41.** For the purposes of this Act, persons and companies discussed in the present Chapter may be granted special customs dispensations, in accordance with existing legislation.

**Article 42.** The payment of customs tariffs, duties and other fees shall be realized in freely convertible currency, even in those cases in which the amount is expressed in national currency, discounting the exceptional cases which may be established by the Executive Committee of the Council of Ministers.

**Article 43.** The Ministry of Finances and Prices, after consulting with the Ministry of Foreign Investment and Economic Cooperation and taking into account the benefits and size of the investment, the recovery of capital and the indications made by the Executive Committee of the Council of Ministers for priority sectors of the economy and the benefits that could be accrued by the national economy, may grant total or partial exemptions, on a temporary basis, or grant the benefits within its jurisdiction, in relation to the special taxation system.

**Article 44.** Joint ventures, the parties to international economic association contracts and totally foreign capital companies are subject to the "Norms for Assessing the Most Significant Assets and Liabilities" issued by the Ministry of Finance and Prices. Such persons can freely determine the accounting system which most suits them, as long as the adopted system conforms to universally accepted accounting principals and meets fiscal demands.

## CHAPTER XIII
## RESERVES AND INSURANCE

**Article 45.1.** Joint ventures, foreign and national investors party to international economic association contracts and totally foreign capital companies are obliged to establish reserves, charged to profits, to cover contingencies that may arise in their operations.

**2.** The procedure for establishing, utilizing and liquidating the reserves foreseen in the previous clause is regulated by the Ministry of Finance and Prices.

**Article 46.** Without detriment to the reserves discussed in the previous Article, joint ventures, foreign and national investors party to international economic association contracts, and totally foreign capital companies may establish other reserves on a voluntary basis in accordance with the regulations of the Ministry of Finance and Prices.

**Article 47.1.** Joint ventures, foreign and national investors who are party to international economic association contracts, and totally foreign capital companies should establish insurance policies with companies authorized by the Ministry of Finance and Prices to operate in the country, for the protection of goods, properties, operations and any other activity or against any risks as necessary, on the basis of premiums and other contractual conditions which are competitive internationally.

**2.** Industrial, tourism or other installations or lands leased by state enterprises or other national organizations are insured by the leases in favor of the lessor, in accordance with the conditions foreseen in the previous clause.

## CHAPTER XIV
## REGISTRY AND FINANCIAL INFORMATION

**Article 48.** Joint ventures, national and foreign investors party to international economic association contracts and totally foreign capital companies before commencing their operations, must be inscribed in the registry maintained on these activities by the Republic of Cuba's Chamber of Commerce, within a period of 30 days following the date of authorization.

**Article 49.1.** Persons and companies mentioned in the present Chapter shall present to the Ministry of Foreign Investment and Economic Cooperation, within a period of 90 days following the end of their fiscal year an annual report of their operations in that period.

**2.** The presentation of an annual report by the persons and companies covered by the present Chapter is independent from their obligations to provide information to the Ministry of Finance and Prices, the corresponding tax administrator and any others that may be established for statistical purposes.

## CHAPTER XV
## DUTY-FREE ZONES AND INDUSTRIAL PARKS

**Article 50.** With the goal of stimulating exports and international trade, the Executive Committee of the Council of Ministers may authorize the establishment of duty-free zones and industrial parks in delimited areas of national territory.

**Article 51.1** Duty-free zones are defined as areas in which, by the decision of the Executive Committee of the Council of Ministers, a special system established covering customs duties, exchange rates, taxation, labor migration, public order, capital investment and foreign trade, and in which foreign investors can participate for the purposes of financial operations, importing, exporting, storage, productive activities or reexporting.

**2.** Industrial parks are defined as areas in which, by decision of the Executive Committee of the Council of Ministers, a special system established covering customs duties, taxation, labor, capital investment and foreign trade, for the development of productive activities with the participation of foreign capital.

**Article 52.** The authorization of foreign investments, if pertinent, may consign particular facilities and incentives offered to foreign investors in the duty-free zones and industrial parks.

**Article 53.** The establishment and norms related to the operation of duty-free zones and industrial parks shall be regulated by special legislation issued for that purpose.

**CHAPTER XVI**
**ENVIRONMENTAL PROTECTION**

**Article 54.** Foreign investment is conceived and stimulated in the context of the country's sustainable development, which implies that during the course of the investment, environmental conservation and the rational use of natural resources shall be carefully undertaken.

**Article 55.** The Ministry of Foreign Investment and Economic Cooperation, in pertinent cases, submits the investment proposals it receives for the consideration of the Ministry of Science, Technology and the Environment, so that the latter may evaluate the investment's suitability from the environmental point of view and determine whether an environmental impact evaluation is required, as well as the suitability of granting the pertinent environmental licenses and establishing a control and inspection program in accordance with current legislation.

**Article 56.1.** The Ministry of Science, Technology and the Environment institutes the measures which may be required to properly control situations that could lead to damage, dangers or risks for the environment and the rational use of natural resources.

**2.** The person or company responsible for the damage or harm is obliged to reestablish the previous environmental situation, repair the material damage and indemnify the injured parties.

## CHAPTER XVII
## SOLUTION OF CONFLICTS

**Article 57.1** The conflicts which may arise in relations between partners of a joint venture, or between foreign investors and national investors party to an international economic association contract, or between partners in a totally foreign capital company in the form of a nominal share corporation shall.be resolved in accordance with the founding documents.

**2.** The same rule applies when the conflict arises between one or more of the foreign partners and the joint venture or totally foreign capital company to which the partner or partners belong.

**Article 58.** Litigation over the execution of economic contracts between joint ventures, foreign investors and national investors party to international economic association contracts or totally foreign capital companies, and state enterprises or other national entities are the jurisdiction of the economic division of the People's Courts established by the Governing Council of the People's Supreme Court.

## SPECIAL PROVISION

Joint ventures, national and foreign investors party to international economic association contracts, and totally foreign capital companies are subject to any regulations that may be established concerning protection against catastrophes and natural disasters.

## TEMPORARY PROVISIONS

**FIRST:** On the date this Act goes into effect, it applies to the existing and operating joint venture and other forms of international economic association. Nonetheless, the benefits granted by Decree-Law No. 50, issued February 15, 1982, shall remain in effect during the whole period in which an existing international economic association is authorized.

**SECOND:** On the date this Act goes into effect, it applies to the requests for foreign investment authorization which are being processed. The Ministry of Foreign Investment and Economic Cooperation and the current applicant shall determine how to proceed.

**THIRD:** The complementary provisions issued by the various central state administrative agencies for the proper application and execution of the norms contained in Decree-Law No. 50 of February 15, 1982 shall continue to be observed on an individual basis, as long as they do not conflict with this Act. The aforementioned agencies, in a period of no more than three months from the date of this Act goes into effect, shall review the aforementioned norms and bring them into harmony with the provisions of the Act.

## FINAL PROVISIONS

**FIRST**: Decree-Law No. 50, "On Economic Association among Cuban and Foreign Entities," issued on February 15, 1982, as well as any other legal provisions contrary to the contents of APPROVED on the floor of the National Assembly of the People's Power, International Conference Center, City of Havana, on the fifth day of the month of September of the year nineteen ninety-five.

(signed) RICARDO ALARCON DE QUESADA

Published in a special issue of the Official Gazette, Number 3, dated September 6th, 1995.

# Insider Information about opportunities in other countries

*Please take the time to read this section.*

*Thank you.*

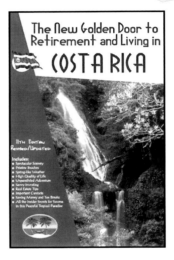

# Live in Nicaragua.com

*The most complete one-of-a-kind guidebook to finding the good life in Central Americas "Sleeping giant" and "Land of opportunity."*

## What the experts are saying about Nicaragua:

"Nicaragua is a HOT new travel destination and expatriate HAVEN" -- *U.S. News and World Report*

"Almost 10,000 Americans have already DISCOVERED Nicaragua and call it their HOME" -- *USA Today*

## Praise for the author:

"This **VISIONARY** work will help anyone thinking of living or making money in Nicaragua. It promises to become a **CLASSIC**." -- *Nicaraguan Institute of Tourism*

"Want to live or Making Money in Nicaragua?  Then **READ** this guidebook." -- *Central America Weekly*

## HOW TO ORDER

**COSTA RICA BOOKS**
**Suite 1 SJO 981. P.O. Box: 025216**
**Miami, FL. 33102-5216**
**E-mail: crbooks@racsa.co.cr**
## Call toll free: 800 365-2342

We accept

or
**www.amazon.com**
**www.liveinnicaragua.com**

# CHAPTER 9

## GETTING THERE, MOVING THERE AND STAYING THERE

### Getting There

The majority of visitors to Cuba come by air and fly into Havana's new modern terminal at **José Martí International Airport**. Cuba has international airports in Havana, Cayo Largo, Varadero, Camagüey, Holguín, Santiago de Cuba and Cienfuegos. **Cubana**, the country's national airline, has regular service to and from Europe. There is a weekly flight from London. There are usually two flights weekly to Cuba from Europe. **Aeroflot**, the Russian airline and **KLM** from Amsterdam both have weekly flights to Havana. **Iberia** offers daily flights from Madrid. **LTU** flies from Germany. **Viasa**, Venezuela's airline, also flies to Cuba.

**Cubana** offers service from Central and South America. There are also flights from nearby countries like the Bahamas (Cubana), Jamaica (Air Jamaica), the Dominican Republic (Cubana), Costa Rica (Lacsa Airlines), from Mexico City and Cancún (Mexicana Airlines and Aeromexico) and Panama (Copa). You can keep up on Cubana's schedules by accessing their website at: http://cubana.cu.

Here is a list of major airline offices in Havana:

**Aeroflot-Russian Airlines** - Tel: 33-3200, Fax: 33-3288 or www.aerofloat.com.

**Air France** - Tel: 66-2642, Fax: 66-2634 or www.airfrance.com

**Air Jamaica** - Tel: 66-2247 Fax 66-2634 or www.airjamaica.com

**COPA** - Tel: 33-1758 Fax: 33-3951

**Cubana Airlines** - Tel: 3-4949

**Grupo Taca** - Tel: 33-3114 Fax: 33-3728 or www.grupotaca.co.cr

**Iberia** - Tel: 33-5041 Fax: 33-5061 or ww.iberia.com

**LTU International Airways** - Tel: 33-3524 Fax: 33-3590 or www.ltu.com

**Mexicana de Aviación** - Tel: 33-3531 Fax: 33-3077 or www.mexicana.com.mx

There are frequent flights from the Canadian cities of Toronto, Montreal and Quebec to Havana, Varadero and Santiago de Cuba. Contact **Air Canada** (416) 925-2311 or **Cubana** (514) 871-1222. Affordable charter flights are also available from Canada. Canadian charters usually fly directly to Havana, Varadero, Cayo Largo, Cienfuegos Camaguey (Playa Santa Lucía), and Holguín (Guardalavaca). Canadians can find low priced flights in the Saturday travel section of most newspapers. Regents Holidays is one of the many Canadian companies flying to Cuba. They have colorful brochures about their packages and charters to Cuba. For further information contact them at 6205 Airport Rd., Bldg. A Suite 200, Mississagua, Ontario L4V 1E1 Tel: (905) 673-3343 Fax: (905) 673-1717 or see www.regentholidays.com.

Several charter and tour companies are currently working out of the US Expatriate Cubans and journalists are the only people permitted to travel to Cuba at present. Others may apply for a visa through the Cuban Interests Section in Washington, D.C. However, you may circumvent the current restrictions by flying from Mexico, the Bahamas, Costa Rica or another country. Once you get there the Cubans will not stamp your passport.

**Destination Cuba** is a new company which offers licensed charter flights and trips from the U.S. to Cuba. To get in touch with them, call **800-493-8426 www.destinationcuba.com**. We recommend their services highly. You may also want to check out **www.cubatravel.com.mx** for reservations from Mexico. *Cuba Update,* a bi-monthly magazine, has information about special tours to Cuba. Contact them at 124 West 23rd Street, New York, NY 10011, Tel: (212) 242-0559.

To see the country, **Cubana de Aviación** offers domestic flights to other points in the country from Havana. They fly to the following cities: Baracoa, Bayamo, Camagüey, Ciego de Avila, Guantánamo, Holguín, Las Tunas, Manzanillo, Nueva Gerona, and Santiago de Cuba. For domestic flights, Cubana's office in Havana is at Calle Infanta, corner Humbolt, Plaza. Tel: 70-5961. For international flights another office is located at Calle 23 No 64, Vedado, Havana, Tel: 78-4961 or 33-4949.

Some adventurous individuals travel to Cuba by sea. Those people travelling this way should contact the harbor master's office before you arrive. give them details about your crew, boat and passengers. Don't forget to do the same when you leave the country. We have an American friend who lived at the Hemingway Marina for over a year. He really enjoyed his stay. What made it even better was the fact that he had a satellite TV system on his yacht. He said watching programs from the States really helped him survive some dull moments.

The **Hemingway Marina** is located at the western end of Havana. It is a self-contained and duty-free port with its own lodging and complete services.

In addition to the **Hemingway Marina**, visitors may anchor their yachts at the **Marina Tarará** (eastern beaches), **Varadero, Marina María La Gorda** in Pinar del Río Province, **Marina Puesto del Sol** (Cayo Largo), **Marina Jagua** (Bay of Cienfuegos), and the **Marina Cayo Guillermo**.

Another friend, who is a famous travel writer, has entered the country several times in the last few years by boat from the United States. He even brought a motorcycle into the country. He didn't have problems except for one time when trying to leave the country. When he was about to leave on a private yacht, he was subjected to a thorough search and asked many questions about what he was doing in Cuba. He was eventually allowed to depart about an hour later after he had politely cooperated with the immigration agents.

# Moving There

One of the most important decisions you will have to make is, what to take and what to leave behind. What you need really depends on your lifestyle. If you absolutely can't do without your modern conveniences from home, then you will end up spending a lot of money on shipping costs and duties. You will also have to get used to the many delays as you wait for your things to clear Cuban customs. For some people, having their own furniture, appliances and other possessions, will help them feel more at home while living abroad. It will also ease adjustment to living in a new country by having familiar objects in their home so they won't be so apt to get homesick.

Once the embargo is lifted, the most inexpensive place to ship your goods will be from Miami since it is the nearest port. You will probably be able to send items by air cargo but will have to pay more. If you are on a tight budget shipping by boat will save you money. All you will have to do is check the Miami phone book to find shipping companies. From Canada or the west coast of the US, you will have to ship overland to Miami to reduce the cost. Before the Castro era there was a daily ferry from Florida to Cuba. If this service is resumed, it will be even easier to transport a vehicle.

Some people feel comfortable without many objects from home, so they will not have to ship all of their belongings. By renting a furnished house or apartment you will eliminate the need of importing your furniture. In the event you will want to stay permanently, you will be able to purchase local furniture or appliances. In any case, you should make an effort to get rid of clutter and don't take what can be easily or cheaply replaced. Talk with other foreign residents to see what they recommend bringing. If you do have to move or return home, you will be glad you didn't bring a lot of things with you.

## Staying There

Tourists from most countries need only a passport which must be accompanied by a tourist card (tarjeta de turista) to enter Cuba. Visas usually cost between $25 and $35 depending where it is purchased. To obtain a tourist card, a round-trip ticket in and out of the country is required. There are also a few forms to fill out. Depending on your country, tourist cards may also be obtained from Cuban consulates, embassies, Cubatur operators, travel agents or from airlines. Check to see which countries require a visa. Note that everyone entering Cuba must have a return-or onward-travel plane ticket.

Tourist cards are usually good for 30 days at a time. Both Tourist Cards and Tourist Visas are renewable for two successive periods or prórrogas of 30 days each. What they do is issue you a new tourist card every month for a period up to six months. This extension is granted at the discretion of Cuban Immigration.

What you have to do is go to the immigration office and present your tourist card, passport and pay $25. Extensions are issued at the Control de Extranjeros immigration office on Calle 20 between 3 and 5 in Miramar.

You can also get extensions at any tourist office or at some hotels. The Hotel Havana Libre, Calle 23 and L, in Vedado has an office where you can renew your papers. If you experience problems, go to the **Ministerio de Relaciones Exteriores** (MINREX), Calzada No. 360 and Avenida de los Presidentes in Vedado, Tel: 30-5031. This government entity is in charge of passports, visas and tourist cards.

It must be pointed out that any foreigner who stays in Cuba for more than 30 days is required to register at the Immigration Office and will need to get an exit permit from an immigration office to leave the country. Furthermore, anyone who stays in Cuba longer than 90 days must have an HIV test. Any individual who tests positive is denied a visa. Also any foreigner who resides legally in Cuba needs a re-entry permit to travel abroad and return to the country. Said permit is usually valid for multiple entries. Multiple entry business visas are also available for certain types of businesses.

Journalists, businessmen and others interested in long-term stays must have a visa. To get one, go to any Cuban consulate. Visitors travelling on a visa must go in person to Cubatur or Immigration for registration the day after they arrive.

Presently there are two residency programs for foreigners. Residency has only been given to foreign partners in joint ventures and to some of their employees. However, you don't need residency to do business in Cuba.

Temporary Residency may be applied for by businessmen and investors who decide to stay in the country to manage their businesses. This type of residency may be applied for through the International Legal Council at 16 Street # 314 in Miramar. The cost is about $150 USD per hour of consultation.

Permanent Residency can be obtained if married to a Cuban citizen. Once you turn in your application, you should not stay in the country for more than two consecutive months until Cuba Immigration grants this status.

Once again, at the present time the U.S. government does not permit its citizens to go directly to Cuba. Journalists, writers, those engaged in academic research and relatives of Cubans are eligible for visas by contacting the **Cuba Interests Section**. They are located at 2630 16th N.W., Washington, D.C. (Tel: 202-797-8609) or 2900 Cathedral Ave., 202-745- 7900. There are a few tour operators who will also be able to help your get a visa if you go on one of their excursions to Cuba.

As we alluded to before, U.S. citizens can get around these stringent regulations by travelling through a third country like the Bahamas, Jamaica, Dominican Republic, Mexico or Costa Rica.

## Customs

Visitors may bring their personal belongings including such items as clothing, fishing equipment, photography equipment, a tape recorder, a radio, a personal computer, a bicycle, a surfboard and other sports gear, gifts up to a value of $100, medicines, toilet articles, 3 liters of any alcoholic beverages and up to 200 cigarettes. New items which don't fit into these categories are subject to a 100% customs duty up to a maximum of $1000. For importing greater amounts contact a Cuban consulate. We suggest you also contact a Cuban consulate about items which one cannot bring to Cuba and rules for carrying large amounts of cash.

Here is a list of Embassies outside of Cuba to answer your questions and help you with your paper work.

**Australia**
PO Box 1412
Maroubra
NSW 2035
Tel: (61) 2-9311-4611
Fax: (61) 2-9311-1255

**Austria**
Eitelbergergasse 24
A11 30 Wien
Tel: (1) 877-8198

**Canada**
388 Main St.
Ottawa K1S 1E3
Tel: (613) 563-0141
Fax: 540-2066

**France**
16 Rue de Presles
75015 Paris
Tel: 4567-5535
Fax: 4566-4635

**England**
15 Grape St.
WC2H 8DR
Tel: 071-240-2488
Germany
Stavanger Strasse 20
10439 Berlin
Tel: 49-30-9161-1810

**Italy**
Via Licinia
00153 Roma
Tel: (6) 575-5984

**Netherlands**
Prins Mauritslaan 6
2582 LRR The Hague
Tel: (2) 371-5766

**Mexico**
Presidente Masarik 554
Colonia Polanco,
Mexico 5 DF
Tel: (5) 259-0045

**Spain**
Paseo de La Havana 194
Madrid
Tel: 910 458-2500

**Switzerland**
Seminarstrasse 29
3006 Bern
Tel: (31) 444-834/835

**United** States
Cuban Interests Office
2630 16th St. N.W.,
Washington, DC 20009
Tel: (202) 797-8518, 797-8609 Fax: (202) 797-8512

The following offices of the Cuban Tourist Bureau are located abroad. They may be more helpful than the consulates or embassies.

**Argentina**
Oficina de Promoción e Información Turística de Cuba
Paraguay 631, 2 piso
Buenos Aires, Capital Federal
Tel: (11) 4326-57810
Fax: (11) 4326-3325
E-mail; oturcuar@tournet.com.ar

**Brazil**
Av. Sao Luis 50-39 Andar,
CEP 01046
Sao Paolo, SP
Tel: (11) 259-3044,
Fax: (11) 258-8818

**Canada**
Cuban Tourist Board
55 Queen St East, Suite 705
Toronto, Ontario, M5H 1R5
Tel: (416) 362-0700
Fax: (416) 362-6799
E-mail: cuba.tbtor@sympatico.ca

**France**
Office de Promotion et Information Touristique de Cuba
24 Rue du Quatre Septembre
Paris 75002
Tel: (145) 389-010
Fax: (145) 389-930

**Germany**
Steinweg 2
600 Frankfurt Main 1
Tel: 069-28-8322
Fax: 069-29-6664
E-mail: gocuba@compuserve.com

**Italy**
Via General Fara 30
Terzo Piano
20124 Milano, Italy
Tel: (02) 6698-1463
Fax: (02) 6738-0725
E-mail: uffcioturisticodicuba@interbusiness.it

**México**
Oficina de Promoción e Información Turística de Cuba
Insurgentes Sur 421, esq. Aguascalientes
Complejo Aristos, Edificio B, Local 310
México, DF 0610
Tel: (5) 255--5897
Fax: (5) 255-5866
E-mail: otcumex@mail.internet.cma.net

**Russia**
Hotel Belgrado, Moscow
Tel/fax: (095) 243-0383

**Spain**
Oficina de Promoción e Información Turística de Cuba
Paseo de La havana 28, no 1
Madrid 28036
Tel: (91) 411-3097
Fax: (91) 564-5804

**United Kingdom**
161 High Holborn
London WC1 V6PA
Tel: (171) 836-3606
Fax: (171) 240-6655
E-mail: cubatouristboard.london@virgin.net

The following countries have embassies/consulates in Havana.

**Argentina**: Calle 36 No. 511, between 5 & 7 Ave, Tel: 24-2972, Fax; 24-2140.

**Austria**: Calle 4 No. 101, corner of 1 Ave Tel: 24-2394, Fax: 24-1235.

**Belgian**: Ave 5 No. 7408 at Ave 76 in Miramar Tel: 24-2410, Fax:24-1318.

**Bolivia**: Calle 26 No. 109, between 1 & 3 Ave Tel: 33-2127/2426.

**Brazil**: Calle 16 No. 503, between 5 & 7 Ave Tel: 24-2139, Fax; 24-2328.

**Canada**: Calle 30 No. 518, between 5 and 7, Miramar Tel: 24-2516, Fax: 24-2516.

**Chile**: Avenida 33 No. 1423, Miramar, Tel: 24-1222, Fax: 24-1694.

**China**: Calle C No. 317, between 13 and 15, Vedado, Tel: 33-3005, Fax: 33-3092.

**Colombia**: Calle 14, No. 515, Miramar, Tel; 24-1246, Fax: 24- 24-1249.

**Costa Rica**: Calle 46, No. 306, Miramar, Tel: 24-6937.

**Denmark**: Paseo de Martí, No. 20, Havana Vieja, Tel: 33-8128, Fax: 33-8127.

**Ecuador**: Avenue 5A No. 4407 between 44 & 46 Streets (Tel: 33-2024/2820).

**Finland:** Calle 140, No. 3121, between 21 and 23. Miramar, Tel:/Fax: 24-0793.

**France:** Calle 14 No. 312, between 3 & 5 Avenues Tel: 24-2143, Fax: 24-2317.

**Germany:** Calle 13 No 652, Vedado Tel: 33-2460, Fax: 33-1586.

**Greece:** Avenue 5, No. 7802, Miramar, Tel: 24-2995, Fax: 24-1784.

**Hungry:** Calle G, No. 458, Vedado, Tel: 33-3365, Fax: 33-3286.

**India:** Calle 21, No. 202, Corner K, Vedado, Tel: 33-3378, Fax: 33-3287.

**Italy:** Paseo No. 606, between 25 & 27, Vedado, Tel: 33-3378.

**Jamaica:** Avenida 5, No. 3608, between 36 and 36A, Miramar, tel: 24-2908.

**Japan:** Calle N No. 62 at Calle 15, Tel: 33-3454, Fax: 33-3172.

**Mexico:** Calle 12 No. 518, between 5 and 7 Ave, Tel: 24-2909, Fax: 24-2719.

**Netherlands:** Calle 8, No. 307, Miramar, Tel: 24-2511, Fax: 24-2059.

**Nicaragua:** Calle 20, No.709, Miramar, Tel: 24-1025, Fax: 24-6323.

**Norway**: Paseo de Martí, No. 20, Havana Vieja, Tel: 33-8128, Fax: 33-8127.

**Panamá**: Calle 26, No.109, Miramar, Tel: 24-1673, Fax: 24-1674.

**Perú**: Calle 36, No. 109, between 1 & 3 Avenues, Miramar Tel: 24-2474, Fax: 24-2636.

**Poland**: Avenida 5, No. 4407, Miramar, Tel/Fax: 24-1323.

**Portugal**: Avenida 5, No. 6604, Miramar, Tel: 24-2871, Fax: 24-2593.

**Romania**: Calle 21, No. 307, Vedado, Tel: 33-3325, Fax: 33-3324.

**Russia**: 5 Avenue, No.6402 between 62 & 66, Tel: 24-1749, Fax: 24-1074.

**Spain**: Cárcel No. 51, corner of Zulueta, Old Havana Tel: 33-8025, Fax: 33-8006.

**Sweden**: Avenida 31A, No. 1411, entre 14 and 18, Miramar, Tel: 24-2563, Fax: 24-1194.

**Switzerland**: Avenue 5, No. 2005, Miramar, Tel: 24-2611, Fax: 24-1148.

**Turkey**: Calle 20, No. 301, Miramar, Tel: 24-2933, Fax: 24-2899.

**United Kingdom**: Calle 34, No 708, Miramar: Tel:24-1771, Fax: 24-1772.

**United States**: Calzada, between Streets L & M, Vedado, Tel: 33-4401, 33-3551, 33-3559.

**Uruguay**: Calle 14, No 506, between 5 & 7 Ave, Miramar Tel: .24-2311, Fax: 24-2246.

**Venezuela**: Street 36A, No 704, between 7 & 42, Miramar, Tel: 24-2662, Fax: 24-2773

**Vietnam**: Avenue 5, No. 1802, Miramar, Tel: 24-1042, Fax: 24- 1041.

**Yugoslavia**: Calle 42, No. 115, Miramar, Tel: 24-2982, Fax: 24-2982.

**Zimbabwe**: Avenida3, No. 1001, Miramar, Tel: 24-2137, Fax: 24-2720.

# CHAPTER 10

## USEFUL INFORMATION

## M.R.T.A. Overseas Retirement Adaptability Test

Using the figures 1 (below average), 2 (average) or 3 (above average), ask yourself the following questions and rate your answer accordingly. Couples should take the test separately. as you take the test, write your selected num,bers down, then add them together. When completed, refer to the Score Comments Box at the bottom of this page.

1) Open to new adventures
      select one: 1 2 3
2) Flexible in yourlifestyle
      select one: 1 2 3
3) Enthusiastic to new things in a new and different culture
       select one: 1 2 3
4) Able to make and enjoy new friends:
      select one: 1 2 3
5) Willing to learn at least basic phrases in a new language
      select one: 1 2 3
6) Healthy enough mentally and physically not to see family, friends and favorite doctor for occasional visits
      select one: 1 2 3
7) Confident enough to be in a "minority" position as a foreigner in a different culture
select one: 1 2 3
8) Independent and self-confident enough not to be influenced by negative and ofter ignorant comments against a possible move to a foreign country
      select one: 1 2 3
9) Patient with a slower pace of lifes
      select one: 1 2 3
10) Usually optimistic
      select one: 1 2 3
11) Eager to travel to a new country
      select one: 1 2 3
12) Open mind to a dealing with a different type of bureaucracy
      select one: 1 2 3
13) Understand enought to look at things in adifferent light without being critical and accepting the differences
      select one: 1 2 3
14) Finacintially stable without needing to work
      select one: 1 2 3

| Score Comments: | |
| --- | --- |
| Your Score | Evaluation |
| 37-45 | Great move abroad |
| 30--36 | Will have a few problems |
| 22-32 | Some problems but possible |
| Less than 22 | Forget it, stay home! |

Test taken from the book "Mexico Retirement Travel Assistance." To order wrtie M.R.T.A., 6301 S. Squaw Valley Rd., Suite 23, Pahrump, NV 89648-7949

# 22 Things Every Prospective Expatriate Should Know
## by Shannon Roxborough

Whenmoving to aforeign country, making adequate pre-departure preparations is essential. Here are some tips to make your international move easier.

1) Be sure to undergo a complete medical check-up before leaving to aovid dealing with amajor health issue overseas.

2) Take one or more advance trips to your destination to familiarize yourself. It's worth the investment.

3) Take the appropriate documents on the advcance trip to start the immigration paperwork. Consulate personnel in the country can secure the visa and residency permmit more efficiently that those working thousands of miles away.

4) if you have dependent children, in your pre-departure research, be thorough in seeking the availibility of education in your host country.

5) Make sure you and your family understand the country's culture so that they know what will be accepted in terms of volunteer and leisure activities at your new home.

6) In case of emergencies, make sure you know good health-care providers and how to contact them.

7) use a travel agency for booking en-route travel so you may search for low-cost fares

8) Check into purchasing round-trip tickets for en-route travel. They may be less expensive that one-way. And the return may be used for other travel.

9) Remember the sale of your stateside home increases tax cost due to lost interest deduction.

10) Cancel regular servixces and utilities. Pay the closing bill for garbage collecting, telephone, electricity, water, gas, cable TV, newspapers, magazines (or send them a change of address), memberships such as library and clubs, store accounts (or notify them that your account is inactive), and credit or check - cashing cards that will not be used.

11) Leave forwarding address with the Post office or arrange for a mail forwarding service to handle all your U.S. mail.

12) Give notice to your landloard or make applicable arrangements for the sale of your home.

13) Havre jewelry, art, or vaulables properly appraised, especially if they will be taken abroad. Register cameras, jewelery and other similar items with customs so that there will be no problem when reentering the U.S.

14) make sure a detailed shipping inventory of househld and personal effects is in the carry-on luggage and a copy is at home with a designated representative.

# APPENDIX
## Recommended Reading

*Adventures Abroad*, by Allene Symons and Jane Parker. Gateway Books. Much insight into retirement outside the U.S. Indispensable for anyone interested in residing abroad.

*Cuba Handbook*, by Christopher Baker. Moon Publications 5855 Beaudry St., Emeryville, CA 94608. Written by the winner of the 1995 Benjamin Franklin Award for best travel guide, this comprehensive work is by far the most outstanding guidebook ever written about travelling in Cuba. Virtually everything is covered within its 715 pages. Don't leave home without this great book. To order contact www.travelguidebooks.com.

*Cuba*, by David Stanley. Lonely Planet Publications, Oakland, Ca 1997. At 400 pages this is the second-best travel guide on the subject.

*Cuba*, by Andrew Coe. Lincolnwood: NTC Publishing. Contains good descriptions of Cuba's regions.

*Cuba*, by Adam Kufeld. W.W. Norton & Company, Inc. New York N.Y. A book containing beautiful photographs of Cuba.

*Cuba*: *Official Guide*, by A. Gerald Gravette. The Macmillan Press Ltd. 1988. Outdated but packed with valuable information and good to use for exploring the country.

*Cuba*: *Travellers Survival Kit*, by Simon Calder and EmilyHatchwell. Published by Vacation Work, 9 Park End Street, Oxford, England OX1 1HJ Fax: 0865-790885.

***Cuba Update***, published by the Center for Cuban Studies, 124 West 23rd Street, New York, Ny 10011, Tel; (2120 242-0559; Fax; (212) 242-1937. Reading this publication is an excellent way to keep up on what is happening in Cuba.

***Dictionary of Cubanismos***, by José Sánchez-Boudy. Ediciones Universal, Miami, Florida. This book is written in Spanish and contains a lot of slang and other expressions.

***Escape from America***, by Roger Gallo. Manhattan Loft Publishing Company, 738 East Burnside, Portland, Oregan 97214. It is also available from: http://www.escapeartist.com. This book is a "must read" for anyone who wants to relocate overseas. It has the answers to all of your questions plus profiles the best countries in which to live.

***Fodor's Cuba***, by Fodor's Travel Publications 1996.

***The Freedom Handbook***, a guide to Personal Freedom,Wealth and Privacy. by Charles Freeman. Freedom Publications, P.O. Box 115, St. Helier, Jersey, Channel Islands, via Great Britian. Contains a wealth of useful information for the expat.

***Getting to Know Cuba: A Travel Guide***, by Jane McManus. St. Martin's, New York 1989. Written by a long-time resident of Havana.

***Havana Handbook***, by Christopher Baker. This companion guide to the best-selling Cuba Handbook is the first ever travel guidebook in English devoted exclusively to the Cuban capital. For information contact www.travelguidebooks.com.

***The International Man***, by Douglas Casey. This book is the expatriate's bible to overseas investment. It is out of print but you may be able to find it in a used bookstore or library.

*Insight Guides CUBA*, Houghton Mifflin Company 1996. This fine book offers a very graphic view of Cuba.

*Mexico and Central American Handbook*, Passport Books, Chicago, Il. This annual travel guide has a good chapter on Cuba.

*Mi Moto Fidel: motorcycling through Castro's Cuba*, by Christopher Baker. Another gem written by Mr. Baker. This work is a vivid account of the author's 13,000 km trip around the island. It is full of anecdotes and interesting insights.

*Our Man in Havana*, by Graham Green. Penguin, New York.

*Survival Kit for Overseas Living*, by L. Robert Kohls. Intercultural Press, P.O. Box 700, Yarmouth, Maine 04096. This book is also a 'must read' for anyone thinking about moving outside of the country. We recommend it highly.

*The Old Man and the Sea*, by Ernest Hemingway. Scribner's, New York. The author won the Noble Prize for this classic.

*Trading with the Enemy*, by Tom Miller. Macmillan Publishing Company, New York, NY. Good account of Cuban life in the early 90's.

*Women of the Caribbean*, by Christopher Baker. Beautifully illustrated coffee table book portraying the most gorgeous women from Cuba and Costa Rica. Contact www.travelguidebooks.com.

# Hotels in Other Parts of the Country

**Varadero**

Atabey ....................................................................Tel:6-30-13
Bellamar ................................................................Tel:6-30-14
Cabinas del Sol....................................................Tel:6-30-11
Cuatro Palmas .....................................................Tel:66-7040
Dos Mares .............................................................Tel:6-27-02
El Caney ................................................................Tel:6-39-14
Gaviota Tourist Complex...................................Tel:66-7240
International ..........................................................Tel:66-7038
Kawama Tourist Complex..................................Tel: 66-7156
Melía Varadero ....................................................Tel:66-7013
Melia Las Américas ............................................Tel:66-7600
Puntarena ..............................................................Tel:6-39-17
Oasis.......................................................................Tel:66-7380
Sol Palmares.........................................................Tel:66-7009
Siboney ..................................................................Tel:66-7500
Tuxpán ...................................................................Tel:66-7560
Villa Arenas Blancas...........................................Tel:6-26-38
Villa Barlovento...................................................Tel:66-7140
Villa Caleta ...........................................................Tel:66-7080
Villa Caribe ..........................................................Tel:6-33-10
Villa Punta Blanca...............................................Tel:6-39-16
Villa Los Cocos.....................................................Tel:6-25-22
Villa Tortuga ........................................................Tel:6-22-43
Villa Sotavento ....................................................Tel:6-29-53

**Playas del Este**

Hotel Atlántico, Santa María del Mar ..................Tel:2506
Itabo..............................................................................Tel:2580
Tropicoco ....................................................................Tel:2531
Villa Bucanero...........................................................Tel:65-6332

## Pinar del Río
Motel Los Jasmines.............................................Tel:8293-265
La Ermita, Viñales..............................................Tel:829-3204
Villa Soroa, one of the country's best..............Tel:82-2041
Ranco San Vicente, near caves.........................Tel:9-32-01
Pinar del Río .....................................................Tel:83-460

## Cayo Largo
Villa Coral .........................................................Tel:7-94215
Isla del Sur .......................................................Tel:7-94215
Villa Capricho....................................................Tel:7-94215

## Matanzas
Hotel Louvre.....................................................Tel:4047
Hotel el Valle ....................................................Tel:5-3300

## Cienfuegos
Jagua, Punta Gorda..........................................Tel:5757
Rancho Luna .....................................................Tel:48120
Hotel Playa Girón.............................................Tel:4110

## Villa Clara
Santa Clara Libre...............................................Tel:2-7548
Hotel Lake Habanilla, fishing...........................Tel:8-6932
Los Canayes, outside of Santa Clara ................Tel:4512

## Trinidad
Motel Las Cuevas..............................................Tel:4013
Ancón ...............................................................Tel:4011
Costa Sur..........................................................Tel:2504

## Camagüey
Camagüey .........................................................Tel:7-1970
Gran Hotel ........................................................Tel:9-2093

### Guardalavaca
Hotel Guardalavaca................................................Tel: 3-0221
Atlantico ................................................................Tel:30280

### Santiago de Cuba
Santiago de Cuba ..................................................Tel:4-262634
Balcón del Caribe .................................................Tel:9-1506
Las Américas.........................................................Tel:4-2011
Versalles................................................................Tel:9-1014
Bucanero Beach Resort (near Santiago).............Tel: 2-8130
Villa Daiquirí Resort(near Santiago) ..................Tel:5-4016

### Guantánamo
Guantánamo .........................................................Tel:32-6015

### Santa Clara
Motel Los Caneyes .................................................Tel:4512
Santa Clara Libre .................................................. Tel: 2-7548

### Isla de La Juventud
El Colony Hotel, Nueva Geron...........................Tel:2-3512

### Santa Lucía
Mayanabo Hotel ..................................................Tel:322-3-6184

# IMPORTANT SPANISH PHRASES AND VOCABULARY

You should know all of the vocabulary below if you plan to live in Cuba.

| | |
|---|---|
| What's your name? | ¿ Cómo se llama usted? |
| Hello! | ¡Hola! |
| Good Morning | Buenos días |
| Good Afternoon | Buenas tardes |
| Good night | Buenas noches |
| How much is it? | ¿Cuánto es? |
| How much is it worth? | ¿Cuánto vale? |
| I like | Me gusta |
| You like | Le gusta |
| Where is...? | ¿Dónde está...? |
| Help! | ¡Socorro! |
| What's the rate of exchange | ¿Cuál es el tipo de cambio? |

| | | | |
|---|---|---|---|
| I'm sick | Estoy enfermo | Sunday | domingo |
| | | Monday | lunes |
| where | dónde | Tuesday | martes |
| what | qué | Wednesday | miércoles |
| when | cuándo | Thursday | jueves |
| how much | cuánto | Friday | vienes |
| how | cómo | Saturday | sábado |
| which | cuál or cuáles | month | mes |
| why | por qué | January | enero |
| | | February | febrero |
| now | ahora | March | marzo |
| later | más tarde | April | abril |
| tomorrow | mañana | May | mayo |
| tonight | esta noche | June | junio |
| yesterday | ayer | July | julio |
| day before | | August | agosto |
| yesterday | anteayer | September | septiembre |
| day after | | October | octubre |
| tomorrow | pasado mañana | November | noviembre |
| week | la semana | December | diciembre |

| | | | |
|---|---|---|---|
| spring | primavera | right | correcto |
| summer | verano | wrong | equivocado |
| fall | otoño | full | lleno |
| winter | invierno | empty | vacío |
| | | early | temprano |
| north | norte | late | tarde |
| south | sur | best | el mejor |
| east | este | worst | el peor |
| west | oeste | | |
| | | I understand | comprendo |
| left | izquierda | I don't | |
| right | derecha | understand | no comprendo |
| easy | fácil | Do you speak | |
| difficult | difícil | English? | ¿Habla usted |
| big | grande | | inglés? |
| small | pequeño, | hurry up! | ¡apúrese! |
| | chiquito | O.K. | está bien |
| a lot | mucho | excuse me! | ¡perdón! |
| a little | poco | Watch out! | ¡cuidado! |
| there | allí | | |
| here | aquí | open | abierto |
| nice, pretty | bonito | closed | cerrado |
| ugly | feo | occupied | |
| old | viejo | (in use) | ocupado |
| young | joven | free (no cost) | gratis |
| fat | gordo | against the | |
| thin | delgado | rules or law | prohibido |
| tall | alto | exit | la salida |
| tired | cansado | entrance | la entrada |
| bored | aburrido | stop | alto |
| happy | contento | breakfast | el desayuno |
| sad | triste | lunch | el almuerzo |
| expensive | caro | dinner | la cena |
| cheap | barato | cabin | la cabina |
| more | más | bag | la bolsa |
| less | menos | sugar | el azúcar |
| inside | adentro | water | el agua |
| outside | afuera | coffee | el café |
| good | bueno | street | la calle |
| bad | malo | avenue | la avenida |
| slow | lento | beer | la cerveza |
| fast | rápido | market | el mercado |

| English | Spanish | Number | Spanish |
|---|---|---|---|
| ranch | la finca | 0 | cero |
| doctor | el médico | 1 | uno |
| egg | el huevo | 2 | dos |
| bread | el pan | 3 | trés |
| meat | el carne | 4 | cuatro |
| milk | la leche | 5 | cinco |
| fish | el pescado | 6 | seis |
| ice cream | el helado | 7 | siete |
| salt | la sal | 8 | ocho |
| pepper | la pimienta | 9 | nueve |
| post office | el correo | 10 | diez |
| passport | pasaporte | 11 | once |
| waiter | el salonero | 12 | doce |
| bill | la cuenta | 13 | trece |
| | | 14 | catorce |
| blue | azul | 15 | quince |
| green | verde | 16 | diez y seis |
| black | negro | 17 | diez y siete |
| white | blanco | 18 | diez y ocho |
| red | rojo | 19 | diez y nueve |
| yellow | amarillo | 20 | veinte |
| pink | rosado | 30 | treinta |
| orange | anaranjado | 40 | cuarenta |
| brown | café, castaño | 50 | cincuenta |
| purple | morado, | 60 | sesenta |
| | púrpura | 70 | setenta |
| | | 80 | ochenta |
| | | 90 | noventa |
| | | 100 | cien |
| | | 200 | doscientos |
| | | 300 | trescientos |
| | | 400 | cuatrocientos |
| | | 500 | quinientos |
| | | 600 | seiscientos |
| | | 700 | setecientos |
| | | 800 | ochocientos |
| | | 900 | novecientos |
| | | 1000 | mil |
| | | 1,000,000 | un millón |

\* If you want to perfect your Spanish, we suggest you purchase our best-selling Spanish book, "The Costa Rican Spanish Survival Course", and 90-minute cassette mentioned in Chapter 5. It is a one-of-a-kind pocket-sized course designed for people who want to learn to speak Spanish the Costa Rican way.

# Understanding the Metric System

If you plan to live in Cuba, it is in your best interest to understand the metric system. Since you probably didn't study this system when you were in school and it is almost never used in the U.S., you could become confused.

The conversion guide below will help you.

| To Convert: | To: | Multiply by: |
| --- | --- | --- |
| Centigrade | Fahrenheit | 1.8 then add 32 |
| Square km | Square miles | 0.3861 |
| Square km | Acres | 247.1 |
| Meters | Yards | 1.094 |
| Meters | Feet | 3.281 |
| Liters | Pints | 2.113 |
| Liters | Gallons | 0.2642 |
| Kilometers | Miles | 0.6214 |
| Kilograms | Pounds | 2.205 |
| Hectares | Acres | 2.471 |
| Grams | Ounce | 0.03527 |
| Centimeter | Inches | 0.3937 |

# More Useful Addresses

Bus Reservations
Street 21 Y 24
Vedado, Havana

Chamber of Commerce
Street 21, No. 661
Vedado, Havana
Tel: 30-3356

Cubana Airlines
Street 23, No. 64
between Infanta and P.
Vedado, Havana

Cubatur
La Rampa (Street 23)
No. 156
Vedado, Havana
Tel: 32-4521

Havanautos
Capri Hotel
21 between N and O
Vedado, Havana
Tel: 32-0511

Havana Tour
Street 2 no. 17
Between Ave. 1 & 3
Tel: 22-8273

Hermanos Ameijeiras
Hospital
San Lazaro 701, Havana
Tel; 79-8531

INTUR
National Institute of
Tourism
Avenue de Malecón and
Street G
Havana 4, Cuba
Tel: 511-238-INTCU

Ministry of Foreign Trade
Minesterio del Comercio
Infanta 16
Havana, Cuba

Medical Center
Clínica Cira Garcia
Miramar, Havana
Tel: 70-9566

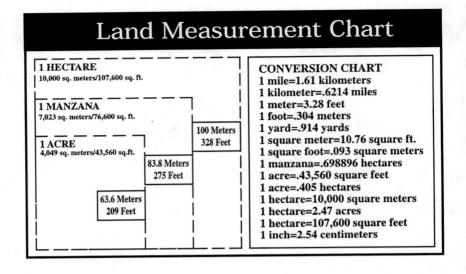

# Land Measurement Chart

**1 HECTARE**
10,000 sq. meters/107,600 sq. ft.

**1 MANZANA**
7,023 sq. meters/76,600 sq. ft.

100 Meters
328 Feet

**1 ACRE**
4,049 sq. meters/43,560 sq.ft.

83.8 Meters
275 Feet

63.6 Meters
209 Feet

**CONVERSION CHART**
1 mile=1.61 kilometers
1 kilometer=.6214 miles
1 meter=3.28 feet
1 foot=.304 meters
1 yard=.914 yards
1 square meter=10.76 square ft.
1 square foot=.093 square meters
1 manzana=.698896 hectares
1 acre=.43,560 square feet
1 acre=.405 hectares
1 hectare=10,000 square meters
1 hectare=2.47 acres
1 hectare=107,600 square feet
1 inch=2.54 centimeters

## TIME

Eastern Standard Time like the rest of the Caribbean and New York. From May to October there is Daylight Savings Time.

## ELECTRICITY

Current used in Cuba is 110 volts and sixty cycles. The same as Canada and U.S. Plugs are American type. Some electric shaver plugs can be 220 volts. A small adapter may have to be used for European appliances such as razors or hairdryers. Power cuts occur often and can harm sensitive equipment like computers.

## CANADIANS

If you are Canadian, non-resident living in Cuba, you should think about receiving the *Canadian Resident Abroad-Update Newsletter*.

To get a free subscription, contact Canadian Residents Abroad Inc., 305 Lakeshore Road East, Oakville, Ontario, Canada L6J 1J3. Tel/Fax 905-842-98141.

# Highway Signs

PESO MAXIMO
LOAD LIMIT

NO
NO PEDESTRIANS

LIMITE
PARKING LIMIT

UNA HORA
ONE-HOUR PARKING

NO
NO LEFT TURN

NO
NO U TURN

NO
NO PARKING

CONSERVE SU DERECHA
KEEP RIGHT

INSPECCION
INSPECTION

NO
NO TRUCKS

PEATONES A SU IZQUIERDA
PEDESTRIANS FACE TRAFFIC

MAXIMA
SPEED LIMIT (IN K.P.H.)

CONTINUA
CONTINUOUS TURN

NO
NO BICYCLES

NO REBASE
NO PASSING

ANCHO LIBRE
HORIZONTAL CLEARANCE

CIRCULACION
USE RIGHT LANE

NO
DO NOT ENTER

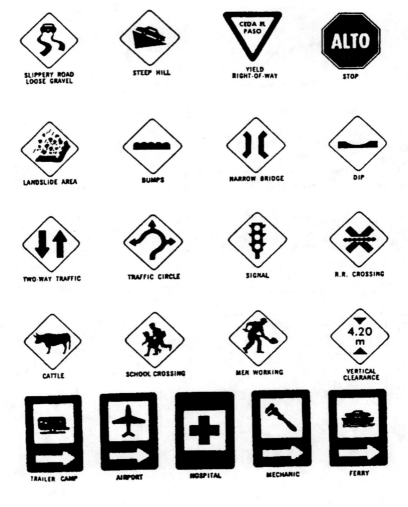

Abierto-open
Aduana-customs
ALTO-stop
Autopista-tollroad or freeway
Bajada-downgrade
Camino Angosto-narrow road
Camino En Reparición-Road under repair
Camino Resbaloso-slippery road
Camino Sinuoso-winding road
Ceda El Paso-yield the right of way
Cerrado-closed
Conserve Su Derecha-keep right
Cruce de Caminos-intersection
Cuidado Con El Ganado-watch out for cattle
Cuidado Con el Tren-watch out for train
Cuota,Peaje-toll road
Curva Peligrosa-dangerous curve
Derrumbe-slide
Despacio-slow
Desviación-detour
Doble Circulación, Doble Vía-two way traffic
Estacionmiento-parking lot
Límite-limit
Maneje Con Cuidado-Drive carefully
No Hay Paso-road closed
Reduzca Su Velocidad-slow down
Peatones-pedestrians
Prohibido La Vuelta a La Derecha-no right turn
Prohibido la Vuelta a La Izquierda-no left turn
Salida-exit
Tránsito-traffic
Velocidad Máxima-maximum speed

# Distance in Kilometers

| | Pinar del Rio | Soroa | Viñales | Ciudad Havana | Varadero | Guamá | Cienfuegos | Santa Clara | Trinidad | Camagüey | Santa Lucia | Holguín | Guardalavaca | Santiago de Cuba |
|---|---|---|---|---|---|---|---|---|---|---|---|---|---|---|
| Pinar del Rio | | 107 | 25 | 178 | 316 | 335 | 512 | 476 | 630 | 746 | 926 | 947 | 1002 | 1143 |
| Soroa | 107 | | 132 | 76 | 216 | 233 | 412 | 376 | 530 | 646 | 826 | 847 | 902 | 1043 |
| Viñales | 25 | 132 | | 203 | 343 | 360 | 539 | 503 | 657 | 773 | 953 | 974 | 1029 | 1170 |
| Ciudad Havana | 178 | 76 | 203 | | 140 | 157 | 336 | 300 | 454 | 570 | 750 | 771 | 826 | 967 |
| Varadero | 316 | 216 | 343 | 140 | | 140 | 186 | 196 | 261 | 466 | 645 | 667 | 722 | 827 |
| Guamá | 335 | 233 | 360 | 157 | 140 | | 120 | 143 | 297 | 413 | 593 | 614 | 669 | 810 |
| Cienfuegos | 512 | 412 | 539 | 336 | 186 | 120 | | 68 | 75 | 338 | 518 | 539 | 594 | 735 |
| Santa Clara | 476 | 376 | 503 | 300 | 196 | 143 | 68 | | 154 | 270 | 450 | 471 | 526 | 667 |
| Trinidad | 630 | 530 | 657 | 454 | 261 | 297 | 75 | 154 | | 252 | 432 | 453 | 508 | 649 |
| Camagüey | 746 | 646 | 773 | 570 | 466 | 413 | 338 | 270 | 252 | | 180 | 197 | 252 | 398 |
| Santa Lucia | 926 | 826 | 953 | 750 | 645 | 593 | 518 | 450 | 432 | 180 | | 377 | 432 | 578 |
| Holguín | 947 | 847 | 974 | 771 | 667 | 614 | 539 | 471 | 453 | 197 | 377 | | 55 | 191 |
| Guardalavaca | 1002 | 902 | 1029 | 826 | 722 | 669 | 594 | 526 | 508 | 252 | 432 | 55 | | 261 |
| Santiago de Cuba | 1143 | 1043 | 1170 | 967 | 827 | 810 | 735 | 667 | 649 | 398 | 578 | 191 | 261 | |

To convert kilometers to miles, multiply by .6 which gives an approximate equivalent.

# INDEX

# NOTES